100 Walls To Be Broken

How To Break The Limits Of Your Mind And Your Heart

Award-winning Author
Kateryna Armenta

Library of Congress Control Number: 2023914703

Print ISBN: 979-8-35071-679-5 eBook 979-8-35092-439-8

This book is dedicated to:
All brave people who support and fight for freedom:
freedom of mind, freedom of heart, freedom
of home, and freedom of country.

CONTENTS

INTRODUCTION

Hello, dear reader, and thank you for choosing this book.

At one point in your life, you, like me, probably took notice of one of your thoughts and realized some inevitable truth for a second. Or for a moment, you even got scared that one of your thoughts, or a bunch of them, were running your life and everything in it.

I want to start with these words:

"You can knock down the walls on the way to your dream, but the main walls to be knocked over are in your head and your heart. Those walls need to be destroyed first before you can move forward."—**Kateryna Armenta**

Did you read my book, *I Know What You Need To Succeed*? If yes, you know I was trying hard to bring my family from Ukraine to the United States due to the war and my fear for their safety. Great news: my mom, my sister, and my niece were able to come, and now we are working on creating some stability for them here. It is no secret that it is difficult for them, and me.

I started to travel the world at 19 years old, and after that I almost didn't have a home but had a lot of time to grow my personality and break my internal walls.

But what happened after my family came to live with me while Ukraine is fighting still now for its survival? I am about to share with you in this book.

Before I start, I want to say that I love having them here, so don't get me wrong. But only after my family arrived, I realized how many walls of thoughts I had destroyed and how many more I had to pick apart, brick by brick, to shine the light of freedom on my locked mind.

The understanding that dawned on me was so deep and so enlightening that I had to share it with you and help you to destroy the walls that you built for yourself for protection but that ended up creating a cage which you unconsciously but so meticulously patch from time to time without realizing it.

Not with me yet? Or maybe you're thinking, *What is this crazy Ukrainian talking about?*

Stay with me.

My husband is from Mexico, and I have traveled to his hometown a few times. I was amazed and disturbed by how they are building houses there, and granted, I am probably spoiled by American openness and no front yard fences. But this will explain to you so clearly what I mean by walls.

Just like my husband's brother, and a lot of other young people who want to be successful and look successful to others, Mexicans decide to find the best lot for a new house they will build for themselves and their family, just the way they want it. And if you have more dinero, you can buy a lot in the better (richer) neighborhood. And that is what you do. You get the lot and create a picture of what your future house will look like. You get an engineer and draft the best floor plan you can come up with. You think, *I want this house to be full of light and many windows…* But then you think, *It gets so hot, so maybe not as many windows after all.* You are starting to build, and of course, you want your house to be strong, so you pour all the walls in concrete. Your house is almost complete, and you have a front yard and a backyard for your children to play in, but then you realize the outside world is not that safe, or maybe not safe at ALL. You completely enclose your house and yard with 10-foot-high fencing and a heavy metal gate, and for added security, you add barbed wire on top of the fence. You think for a second, *Okay, that is enough. It is absolutely safe and secure. No one will be able to get in.* Then you visit your family members, and while washing your hands, you see an iron grate on the window. Out of curiosity, you check the other windows, and all of them have one. You ask the owner of the house about it, and they say you ought to get some too. So the next morning, you get up and call your builder to install an iron grate on every window.

Now that the house is complete, you are satisfied with your creation, not realizing that you, with your own hands, have built a prison for yourself. The only good is that you can come and go as you please. But it is so comfortable that you don't intend to get out much more than before, and at one point, maybe not at all.

Before we continue to the root of why you need to have this book on your shelf and go back to it several times in your life, or maybe every time one of those thoughts tries to rise up once again, I want to say that the part of Mexico I visited had houses just like I have described that made me feel so much like I was in an expensive prison. If everyone built this way, if entire cities were made with giant buildings without anyone needing to come out of them, I wonder how people could choose to live in prison even if it is the nicest and the most expensive in the world.

Let's get back to our house, just like the one I told you about. From early childhood, we build our own walls: strong, out of concrete, and with an iron grate on every window looking out on the world of possibilities. But this time, it is built in our minds and hearts, and so often unconsciously by us for protection from harsh reality, but more often by our parents who don't know any better and just rebuild their own walls but within our minds and hearts.

These walls will hold you back and keep you scared to come out and get what was meant for you. The walls will keep you stressed and overwhelmed, but at the same time comfortable enough in that known house-prison of yours. Breaking the walls you spent so much time building is even more difficult because every time you come close to one of your walls, it will strike your entire body with a painful taser, and only by getting used to it and pushing through can you break the wall in your mind and your heart.

This book will tell you about 100 walls to break to free yourself and live your life with so much peace of mind and unlimited possibilities. After all, all limitations live within our body and our minds, and that is where we will start.

This book could be read in different ways. Read it all or find the wall you are trying to break to be ready for everything that may come your way.

You can start with one or get to all of them. The stories of others will help you to break your wall as they did theirs.

Don't wait; start reading today to free yourself and start breathing with a full chest of peace, possibilities, and potential.

You are one wall away!

P.S. This book is a unique creation with amazing art pieces by one talented artist. Read more about him at the end of the book.

PART I:
I Walls

"The soul becomes dyed with the colour of its thoughts."
—*Marcus Aurelius,* **Meditations**

We have different types of walls, but "I Walls" usually have the most significant impact on our lives and how we introduce ourselves to the world.

I didn't even realize how many of my walls were broken until my family came to live with me due to the situation in Ukraine, and I started to see the walls I used to have in their minds so clearly. However, I can't help anyone if they don't want to be helped or are not ready for it. As I said, breaking any wall is much more complex than raising it.

The mentality in Ukraine is very different. I grew up in it, and I was taught by my parents what they knew about the world and how we are supposed to live in it. Within 13 years, I broke and destroyed so many walls in my head. The list below is just a few of them.

I stopped worrying about what other people think about me or my way of living.

I cleaned my speech of empty or negative words.

I broke stereotypes of what a woman is supposed to do or be.

I cleared some money walls, like "You have to work hard to make money."

I broke the victim mentality that was passed on to me.

I took responsibility for everything happening in my life.

I could keep on going, but I have a better plan!

I separated the walls into four categories: I, Them, Feelings, and Other. Many of them will grow their roots into each other and support the whole structure of your false house of safety, your self-imposed prison. But once you start breaking one wall, other walls will begin to crumble, and the next one will come down easier every time.

So let's get to those "I Walls" and see how far you can go to free yourself.

I AM NOT GOOD ENOUGH

Oh, I know how big this wall is! Almost everyone runs into this one at least once in their lifetime. This is the most known wall, and we tend to build it in many aspects of our lives.

But here, let's pick apart one that applies to your career or your talent, and we will talk about more specific "I am not good enough" walls in the following chapters.

You want to be an artist, dancer, writer, manager, or business owner, but here comes the wall called "I am not good enough."

The artist will say they are not as good as their favorite artist. The dancer will say they are not as good a ballerina as someone they admire… Well, you get the idea. We are constantly judging ourselves by someone out there who we think is "good enough" by our own standards.

But who created those standards? You did. Can you create a new standard where your talent will fit too?

We so often think we are not good enough, and when we hit this wall, we don't try to do anything. We quit before we even start. We don't want to just try and see if someone will like what we have to share with the world.

Stories To Break The Wall

I can find you a million examples, but I picked a few of my favorites.

I love to dance, and this lady was my idol when I started, not because of her technique but because of her willpower to create her own style of dance in a time when ballet was popular. Her name was Angela Isadora Duncan. She was an American dancer. She learned ballet but was never "good enough" and probably got bored with not having enough freedom in it, so she created her own style and became very popular in Europe.

The next one that caught my eye was Samuel Cox, a.k.a. Mr. Doodle. The guy just likes to make doodles, and has become famous now with his extraordinary approach to art. I wonder whether he thought for a moment if his art was not good enough or if he just was doing what he loves. Impressive!

How To Crack This Wall

Some of these techniques will apply to a lot of other walls, but each wall will have some unique questions that you can ask yourself to start pulling bricks out.

I encourage you to find some stories of others in the profession or talent you think you are not good enough for. Read their stories because when we can prove to ourselves the opposite of what we believe, our wall will weaken even on someone else's example.

Ask yourself these questions:

According to whom am I not "good enough"?

Is this opinion from an authority?

What if they are wrong?

What if what I do is new to the world?

What if this will help to break other people's mental walls?

What if everything works out better than I imagine? Would I try, then?

What if this is better than I think it is?

What will make me feel the opposite?

I AM NOT GOOD ENOUGH AS... [YOUR PERSONAL TITLE]

This wall is much more personal. If the previous wall affects our career choices, this one affects our character overall.

You build this wall, for example, as a young mother when your child is crying, and you have no idea why or how to stop it, and you fall to your knees, saying, "I am not good enough as a mother," and it keeps on building. The next time your child bumps his head, you put another brick on that wall. Then when his grades in school are lower than you expected, you put another one. And then, when your child leaves the nest but is not succeeding as you imagined, you complete the last row on your wall.

We build it as fathers who didn't play with their sons enough or missed a holiday or celebration.

We start to put bricks every time we gain some personal title: father, mother, wife, sister, friend, you name it.

But the reality is that the higher you raise this wall, the worse it gets… by believing it is actually true and acting accordingly, by feeling underappreciated (another wall of feeling), and so on.

Why We Do It

Your past created a deep imprint on your self-esteem. Possibly trauma or overdemanding parents influenced the creation of your walls. In fact, a lot of our walls, or at least the bases for them, are built in our childhood.

Sometimes you do not feel good enough because you're too busy comparing yourself to others, or you're trying to be someone you're not because others are doing it one way. Sometimes the comments or opinions of others play a role in what you think of yourself.

You should aim to be the best version of yourself, including being the best [insert your own title] you can be.

How To Crack This Wall

It is almost a full-time job to watch yourself and be aware of when you put another brick on your wall.

Start by forgiving yourself and anyone who is involved in building this wall. Then answer these questions:

What am I doing or not doing?

Is it something another [insert your title] is doing that activates these feelings?

What action can I take to be good enough?

What makes me think this way?

What will make me feel the opposite?

What one thing will make me good enough?

Where can I start?

I CAN'T START... I'M NOT READY

This wall is usually right next to the first wall we examined or sometimes even in front of it.

There is a different type of being ready. Of course, you can't start your doctor career without the proper degree, but don't put off applying for medical school until you feel "ready."

I want to tell you about a few immigrants I met who weren't great at English but studied and passed the real estate exams and found work just fine. Looking at them, I don't think they thought for a second that they weren't ready because they needed to learn more English. They just started not being ready.

Honestly, I started writing my first book and embarked on all my careers without being ready. I am writing this book not ready! I know that it is impossible to be 100% ready. In fact, you are never prepared even after you have accomplished it. You might feel ready when you do this same thing for the fifth or tenth time. Just then, the realization that you know what you are doing will wash over you. But if you want to grow fast, the time will come when you are not ready again.

Stories To Break The Wall

As told by Finally Family Homes:

"Oprah Winfrey is a successful entrepreneur who started with nothing. As most of us already know, Oprah is one of the wealthiest African Americans of the 21st century and has a net worth of $3 billion; she is arguably one of the most influential women in the world.

"Her incredible success becomes more impressive if we consider that she had a very rough childhood. She is the daughter of an unmarried teenager who worked as a housemaid. Oprah's childhood was surrounded by extreme poverty, and they could not even afford to buy school dresses.

She also faced sexual abuse from her family members, which she discussed with her audiences during a special airing of her show.

"Her debut break was working for a local Black radio station. The station managers were impressed with her passion and oratory skills, which allowed Oprah to work up to bigger radio stations. Eventually, she started appearing on television as well."[1]

Almost every famous person started not being ready but believing they could do or be something better than they are.

So don't overthink this. Just start and see if it works out, and even if not, so what? We are all going to die eventually… so who cares if you fail once? But imagine if you don't fail, and then someone might remember you for generations to come.

How To Crack This Wall

I use these questions a lot for myself because, like so many others, I have the same wall that I have had to break more than once in my life, and I am working on it again.

What if I don't try? What will happen?

What if I do try and fail? What will happen?

What if I try and succeed?

How do I think I can get ready? Would I start right after if I did this one thing?

Would I feel better if I tried knowing I did everything I could?

Or if I don't try and wonder what if it had worked?

---

1 7 Famous Entrepreneurs Who Started Insanely Wealthy With No Experience and What Made Them - Finally Family Homes. 19 July 2022, https://finallyfamilyhomes.org/famous-entrepreneurs/.

I DON'T HAVE ENOUGH TIME

So many of these walls will probably speak to you, and this wall is another popular one for so many of us. Time is an important aspect in everything we do. Especially now, I hear it more than ever.

My clients often say, "I want to be fit, but I don't have time to go to the gym, and I don't have time to eat healthy food," or, "I want to have a high-paying job, but I don't have time to study for it."

But the truth is, we always find time for emergencies, right? Let's say you wanted to get fit but never had time for it, and now your heart is giving in… I am sure you would find time to get yourself to the hospital. This will become a top priority, and I am sure everything else will be moved to the side. We always have time for what is truly important to us.

We need to learn how to prioritize. That is one of the reasons I use a planner to prepare my days, weeks, and years. If you don't decide what is important to you and find time to work on it, nothing will change, and then you will find yourself in an emergency situation… but it might be too late.

Why It Happens

Most people are lazy, and we find some excuse to not do the required work.

I discovered an interesting paradox about time. So often we think, *I need to do this, and it will take, let's say, two hours. But right now I only have 30 minutes, so why should I start if 30 minutes is not enough to complete it?* So instead, you find something else to fill those 30 minutes, like scrolling Facebook, TikTok, or Pinterest. Or you do some other meaningless task, like watching TV, or maybe folding the laundry… why not, right? Because 30 minutes is not enough for what needs to be done.

Think of it this way: we all have 24 hours in our day. But some will do a lot of meaningful and amazing things, and some will do nothing with the same amount of time. I watched single mothers with three children building and running their own businesses, staying connected to the family, and having enough time for self-care. And I asked myself how they were doing it, but they just *do*. They don't think there is not enough time. They find time for everything that matters.

How To Crack This Wall

Decide, finally, what is important to you and start doing it. I could say I don't have time to write a book; I am a busy mom and wife, running my coaching business and helping my husband with his. But instead, I find the time, and if it means getting up earlier or writing after my child goes to sleep, that's okay, because it is important to me right now, and it is my responsibility to find time for it. If I have to say no to some things, that is part of the process of finding time for what matters.

Tools to use:

Planner or journal. Plan your life! All successful people do. If it works for them, it will work for you. If a planner doesn't help you, challenge yourself to achieve a goal you couldn't previously find time for, and do it for 30 days straight. Find time no matter what.

Eliminate all distractions and mindless activities from your day. Leave the most important things. You won't be able to hustle all the time, but try to do some marathons once in a while and see how far you get—you might surprise yourself.

Ask yourself these questions:

What if I died a week from today? Would I find the time now for what is important?

What would my perfect day look like, with enough time for everything I need?

What daily activities can be replaced with something that matters more to me?

What is the best way to find the time I need?

How do other people I admire do it?

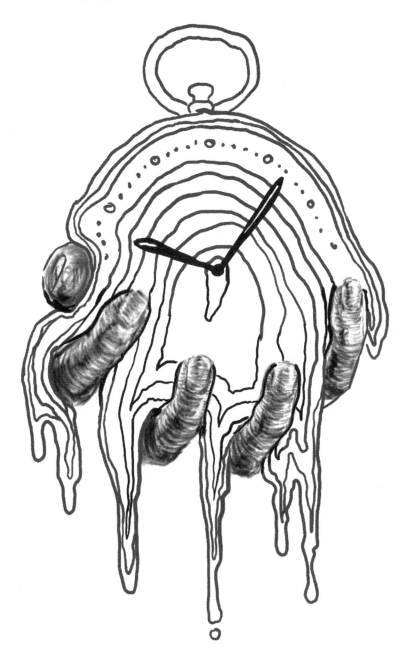

I DON'T HAVE ENOUGH MONEY

All these "not enough" walls fall under the same category, the shortage of something to be happy, prosperous, or successful. But this wall is different. If the others were only thoughts, this one might seem and feel like a reality. You could be on a tight budget and think there is nothing else you could squeeze out. I get it. But do you really need money?

So often, we confuse resources with money. What are you trying to accomplish? There is no shortage of anything in the world, and if you are trying to do something meaningful, maybe the money or resources you need don't have to be yours. I am not telling you to borrow; it could be a way to get what you need, but probably not the best one. You can always find resources from other people: find supporters, find believers in what you want to accomplish, find investors.

Remember, there is never a shortage of anything in the world. You just need to find a way to get it.

Stories To Break The Wall

As told by Business Insider,

"Ed Sheeran is now one of the biggest names in music, but he started off as a struggling artist in London's bustling music scene. The singer would often spend nights sleeping in the London Underground train stations or on top of heating vents. Sheeran now sells out stadiums across the globe and had a net worth in 2022 of $200 million.

"Before the idea for Harry Potter famously came to J.K. Rowling in a dream, the writer was a single mother struggling to pay her rent. She battled depression and other obstacles before becoming one of the most successful female writers. The author's net worth stood at $1.1 billion in 2022."[2]

As you see, lack of money didn't stop them from pursuing their dreams, so stop thinking your lack of money is what is limiting you. Just do what you feel is right, and the opportunity will find you.

How To Crack This Wall

Ask yourself these questions:

Is it really money that I need to pursue my dream?

What can help me move forward?

What resources can I find to help myself?

Who can help me get where I want to go?

Where can I find resources for my dream?

---

2 McDowell, Erin. "19 Famous Figures Who Went from Rags to Riches." Business Insider. Accessed July 30, 2023. https://www.businessinsider.com/millionaires-billionaires-who-came-from-nothing-rags-to-riches-stories-2019-7.

I DON'T HAVE THE RIGHT SKILLS, TALENTS, OR EXPERIENCE

To tell you honestly, 99.99% of successful and talented people didn't have the right skills and experience when they started out. But they probably had an IDEAAAAA. I tried to sing the word on the page here to make you feel the vibe of a light bulb over your head. All successful people had an idea before they knew what to do or create; even the most cutting-edge technology started with a simple idea. Do you think anyone who ever had an idea also had the experience or skills to bring it to fruition?

So if you have an idea, don't worry about everything else. If you don't have a clear idea, start brainstorming. Or even better, hire a life coach!

Stories To Break The Wall

Let me tell you about Jan Koum. I picked him for a reason. In the next sentence, you will understand why. He is a Ukrainian–American billionaire businessman and computer engineer. He is the co-founder and former CEO of WhatsApp, a mobile messaging app that was acquired by Facebook in 2014 for $19.3 billion. According to Forbes, he had an estimated net worth of $13.8 billion as of September 2022, making him one of the richest people in the world.[3]

But his story is both surprising and impressive, according to *Entrepreneur*:

"Koum immigrated to California with his family after leaving a small village in Ukraine. He didn't have much of an education but managed to teach himself the fundamentals of computer science in his spare time. When he was 18, despite his lack of formal education or training, he was able to attract the attention of Yahoo!, where he cut his teeth as

---

3 "Jan Koum." In Wikipedia, July 23, 2023. https://en.wikipedia.org/w/index.php?title=Jan_Koum&oldid=1166659267.

an infrastructure engineer. After a few years working in the then-new computer industry, Koum saw the potential of creating his own app, and launched WhatsApp."[4]

As you read earlier, he sold it for a lot of money. He had little experience and only some skills, but he had a fantastic idea and a burning desire, and voilà.

How To Crack This Wall

Throw this on your wall: I have everything I need to create or get everything I want.

You might not have experience, skills, or talent. But you have the desire to do something or be better. Otherwise, you would not have raised your wall. Talented people doubt themselves, and it is normal at first.

Ask yourself these questions:

What am I really afraid of?

What do I think I need to have to make the first step?

If I get this one thing, will I be ready to take the first step?

What talents do I have?

What skills do I have that might help me here?

---

4 Johansson, Anna. "5 Successful Entrepreneurs Who Started With No Experience But Made Sure They Got It." Entrepreneur, September 13, 2018. https://www.entrepreneur.com/leadership/5-successful-entrepreneurs-who-started-with-no-experience/319971.

I HAVE TOO MUCH STUFF GOING ON

This wall is connected to the time wall. They stand next to each other but have different meanings when we say them to ourselves or others.

When we say "too much going on," somehow it is negative. But isn't it good when the wheels of your life are spinning, and it is not stagnant? This is what life is about. It is supposed to be moving; it is supposed to be changing. Look at nature. SOMETHING CONSTANTLY IS GOING ON, and it is not always good and positive, but it keeps on moving, and it keeps evolving. Sometimes something has to die to feed others, and something has to perish to be reborn again. And all of this is a good thing. That means life is happening.

But the real question is, why do you have that thought? What do you really mean when you say it?

Do you mean you can't add anything additional to your days or weeks? Or do you say that just as a fact or complaint? And if you want to add something important, you just need to decide what is not important and what you can let go.

Why It Happens

We might think for a moment that we have too much going on, but that's what our brain wants us to believe. Sometimes, "too much" is only in our heads because we overthink events that are happening in our life. Our head is preoccupied without us even participating much in it.

But let's say you do have a full plate or a long to-do list. Are you a YES person who can't say NO and always puts someone else first? Maybe it is time to learn what boundaries are and how to set them.

How To Crack This Wall

Ask yourself these questions:

What do I think is stopping me?

When I say that, what do I mean?

What would help me turn it into a positive thing?

What boundaries can I set to create the space I need for more important things?

What are my priorities at this time?

What would I give up to gain what is important?

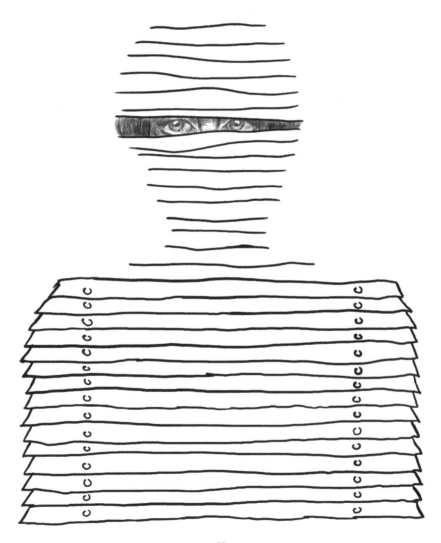

ONE DAY I WILL CHANGE

When we say "one day," most likely, we have no plan for it. We end up building one giant wall of "NO CHANGE." Or we hope it will happen not depending on us but on someone else. What change do you hope for? And when will that one day come?

No time frame makes "one day" not a day in our lifetime. It is almost the same when we say "I will write that book" or "I will lose 70 pounds"… one day. Without urgency, there is no commitment.

If you don't start something now with commitment and consistency, it will not happen. So, decide what exactly you want to change and start working on it. Is it your habits, career, or life? And how do you want it to be different?

Stories To Break The Wall

Walt Disney's first company didn't work out as well as he thought it would. Soon after starting it, he ended up homeless, sleeping in his office and taking showers at the train station. Just a year after opening his doors, Disney was forced to declare bankruptcy.[5] He spent his last dollars on a bus ticket, headed out to Hollywood, and started the company that still bears his name today. His first cartoon character was based on the mouse he used to feed in his first office.

You can change one day, but only if you actively work on it and don't give up.

How To Crack This Wall

Decide for yourself what you want to change and when. Aren't you tired of thinking one day it will happen but doing nothing about it?

---

5 AARP. "Stories of Famous People Who Turned Their Lives Around." Accessed July 30, 2023. https://www.aarp.org/entertainment/celebrities/info-2017/7-famous-people-who-hit-bottom-and-turned-it-around.html.

Make your goal clear and specific, and if it is hard to believe it will happen, start repeating this new thought to yourself. Start telling other people that you are working on it. It will sound something like this:

"I am working on a book, and I will have it out by the end of the year," or, "I am working on losing 40 pounds by the end of April." That way, your brain will start believing that is what you need to do and will start looking for opportunities for it to happen. Then you might be surprised at how fast you will find yourself at the computer typing or at the gym running on a treadmill.

Questions to ask yourself:

How much longer can I live this way?

Would I want to find myself in one year in the same place I am today?

Where can I start to create the change I want?

What exactly would I want to change?

I DON'T LIVE IN THE RIGHT PLACE

If you know me a little bit or at least read the back of the book before you bought it, you probably know I moved to the US from Ukraine. Now I am convinced that this was exactly what had to happen for many reasons. First of all, my journey gave me the story to write, and second, this country gave me the possibility to be a published author and continue to do what I always knew was right. Third, who would have known that by moving to the US years ago, I would be able to save my entire family when the war started? Now tell me that wasn't meant to be.

But that story is not to convince you that you have to move to find yourself—quite the opposite. Changing locations will not have the tremendous impact on your life as you might hope for. Have you heard of the Dilts Pyramid? It has six levels of change; the lower the level, the less influence it will have on your entire life. So now, guess where the environmental level is located? Not on top, not even in the middle. It is the bottom level of the pyramid. The problem is that when we change our location, we still bring our mindset with all the inner walls we created. But as you climb the pyramid to higher levels, the more impact they will have on your life. What are the higher levels? I will leave it for you to find out.

Stories To Break The Wall

With everything I shared above, I am reminded of one of the books I read this year, *Inner Engineering: A Yogi's Guide to Joy*. The author never thought he wasn't in the right place, but he continued his personal growth and development. I thought his story might help you with your wall.

Jagadish Vasudev, known as Sadhguru, was born in India, a spiritually rich country but an economically poor one. He grew up in a typical family with no particular privilege. But neither place of living nor lack of financial support stopped him from pursuing his mission. He is the author of the *New York Times* best-sellers, *Inner Engineering: A Yogi's Guide to Joy* and *Karma: A Yogi's Guide to Crafting Your Destiny*, and a frequent speaker at international forums. Now not only is he not attached to a place, but he also speaks internationally.[6]

How To Crack This Wall

Questions to ask yourself:

What do I think another place can offer that this can't?

What resources do I need in my current location, and where can I find them?

Who can help me here to get closer to my goal?

What am I running from?

6 "Sadhguru." In *Wikipedia*, June 8, 2023. https://en.wikipedia.org/w/index. php?title=Sadhguru&oldid=1159120176.

I DON'T DESERVE NICE THINGS

If you are holding this book and reading about the walls, I am sure you believe in the power of thought. We might not all deserve nice things, but nevertheless, successful people have an abundance of everything. If this is the thought you have, everything else around you will listen to this thought closely, and as a result, you probably will see fewer nice things in your life.

But this wall is a bit different than the others we have talked about. Usually, this is like a bad habit of biting your fingernails when you are nervous. The wall rises up when you see other people around you succeeding but not you, or when something doesn't go as planned. Just like you would bite your fingernail, you tell yourself: "I just don't deserve nice things."

Why It Happens

There are several reasons. Let's go over a few of the most common ones.

Criticism. In the past or present, someone has criticized you for everything you do or don't do. You feel like it doesn't matter what you do; is it never good. You conclude that you don't deserve anything nice.

Self-blame. You haven't forgiven yourself for some actions in the past that you were condemned for or for which you blame yourself. Life happens, and sometimes we make horrible mistakes, but if you can't let it go, several walls will arise, including this one.

Lack of confidence. Confidence is a big topic, and there are a lot of reasons we are not confident in one area or another. A lack of confidence is like concrete support for this wall.

How To Crack This Wall

Forgive yourself and forgive others for everything you have done or everything that was done to you. I know it is easy to say or write, but in reality, this could be the hardest work you have to do for yourself. It will make you cry, but that is okay.

Grow your confidence by doing things that scare you.

Questions to ask yourself:

What do I deserve?

How do I want to live my life?

How do I want to feel about myself?

What do I need in order to forgive myself?

What do I need in order to forgive others?

Whom do I need to forgive?

What thought do I need to believe?

I AM NOT SMART ENOUGH

If after you read the name of this wall, you thought, *Why isn't it at the top with the rest of the "not enough" walls?*, you are probably right. They are in the same category.

Many of us believe that to do something significant, you need to be smart in a specific way. And if we don't have it already, there is no way we can get it. Writing my second book, I still don't think I am smart enough for this. But a lot of other people around me say the opposite.

I love this quote by **Teddy Roosevelt**—*"All the resources we need are in the mind."* And you can figure out how to excavate them or how to put them there.

But if you keep putting bricks on your wall of "I am not smart enough," eventually this is one of the biggest walls you will see, and in everything you try, you will disqualify yourself for not being smart enough.

For years some of my passwords contained the word smart, and I think I started to believe it because I had to tell myself "smart" more than 1,000 times of entering those passwords. But if you do the opposite, that is exactly what you will get. Your brain will not try to prove itself wrong. You should.

Stories To Break The Wall

You probably heard tons of stories about some very successful people who didn't even finish school or who dropped out of college.

You might know this, or you might be surprised to learn that Steve Jobs and Bill Gates dropped out of college. I am sure a lot of people didn't think they were smart enough to do what they have since accomplished.

But maybe being smart is not the most important part in living the life you want to live.

How To Crack This Wall

Ask yourself these questions:

Who do I think is smart enough for what I want to accomplish?

What do I need to do or learn in order to believe I am smart enough for this?

What is my understanding of smart?

What if I don't need to be smart for this?

What quality can I replace it with?

See also the chapter "They Know Better."

I WILL NEVER MAKE MORE THAN...

I taught a class called "Mind Your Own Money." The majority of people who came had this or a similar wall in their self-made prison of thoughts.

One of my big motivations to become a coach was seeing all these women who were at some office job thinking that it was all they could do and that the money they were making was all they were entitled to. I looked at them and could not believe they didn't see what I saw. That is just a wall, an obstacle.

Several clients came to me for those same reasons, so I created the class, in which I would prove that "You can make exactly as much money as you think you can make."

If you read the quote above, I hope you are getting it...

So if you think, *I will never make more than...* whatever your number is, then that is the absolute truth.

Why It Happens

Money is a touchy subject. In our modern world, you can't live without money. So what we think we are worth is a reflection of our self-esteem in a material world.

If you think you can make only $50K, $100K, or whatever your number is, then you probably underestimate your talents and skills or don't know about them altogether. (I didn't know about my talents and skills at one point either.) And to top it all off, you don't value yourself and believe you have nothing special to offer.

How To Crack This Wall

Remember: "You can make exactly as much money as you think you can make."

Figure out what is your next level. Are you making $60K and think this is your limit? Now what will push you out of your comfort zone? Pick a number that makes you uncomfortable, but that you can possibly believe is your new level. Write it down. Maybe it is $75K—a 25% increase, wow, the real deal! Think of as many reasons as you can for why you totally deserve to make this money. If you don't know, ask your good friends and family who support you.

Ask yourself these questions:

What qualities do I have that are worth more than I make?

What is a unique skill that others around me don't have?

What keeps me from making more money?

What can I do to increase my worth or my income?

What investments in myself can help me?

I WILL NEVER BE HAPPY

The wall of unhappiness.

This one is so special because often we think that nothing is our fault and that the outside world is the one who participated in building this wall. No way do we believe it was us, even for a second.

This wall always comes with little decorations that start with the word because… Because no one appreciates me, no one loves me, no one understands me… and any other "because" you can come up with.

But once you comprehend that your happiness depends on you and only you can create it, you can break this wall in a second. Then continue your fight with all the walls around it to free yourself completely.

Why It Happens

As I said, you let your happiness depend on others and completely give your power away. That is usually one of the biggest ones. You usually tell yourself things like *I will be happy when I get this*, or *Someone will do this for me*, or *When this happens*. The worst thing is that even when it does happen, your happiness lasts for a few hours or minutes, or you do not experience it at all. And you go back to square one.

Another big reason is that you haven't learned what self-awareness is. You get attached to your negative emotions, and maybe you compare yourself to others who seem happy without giving yourself a break.

How To Crack This Wall

Tell yourself that your happiness depends on you and no one else. Tell yourself daily until you finally believe it. Watch what your emotions and reactions are. Let negative ones pass by without concentrating on them and getting attached to them.

Stop comparing yourself to others in a judgemental way. Especially now, with all of social media blooming, remember that not everything you see is true. I will share with you a big secret: I have had many clients who felt miserable, but their social media pages were screaming happiness all over.

We all have our own walls to fight, so don't create new ones by coping with someone else's prison.

Ask yourself these questions:

What is happiness for me?

What makes me happy that doesn't depend on others?

When was the last time that I felt happy for real?

What thought passes through my mind when I think about happiness?

What emotions do I usually get stuck with?

What if I choose to be happy?

I DON'T HAVE A CHOICE

If you read my first book, you might remember this wall. This was my WHY to become a coach. The wall was built in my childhood. Many women in my life, including my mother, have this wall. It was so thick, they truly believed that they didn't have a choice in their lives and that it was decided by someone else for them. They had to put their head down and follow the Giant Wall of No Choice.

It can feel awful when you don't seem to have any other options in life. The feeling of being trapped, the anxiety, fear, and a deep level of anger... your mind goes spinning in circles.

But there is always a choice. Even if you are trapped, you have a choice in your spirituality and mindset. The thought goes deeper than that: your entire life is all a choice, even if you don't admit it.

Why It Happens

The root of this wall comes down to not taking responsibility for your life and what is happening to you. Sometimes we think it is easier to give up the power and call ourselves victims. People do it unconsciously, believing they will benefit from it by making others feel sorry for themselves.

But when you really think about anything, there are always three choices: do nothing, do the same thing, or do something different. When we are building this wall in our mind, we usually stick with the first two choices that feel like "NO CHOICE."

Often when we say "NO CHOICE," we mean that we do not want the consequences.

How To Crack This Wall

Be ready to get out of your comfort zone! When we choose to do nothing or do the same as before, it does feel like we have no choice because nothing changes. It requires you to take a step forward and take responsibility for your life. The only way out is to do something different.

The only way out is in: inside, to a more profound understanding of yourself.

The word CHOICE has great power if you use it correctly.

Instead of thinking, *I have no choice,* you can think, *I choose not to do it,* or *I choose to do it another way.* Like this, you don't give your powers away to "No Choice."

Ask yourself these questions:

What can I do differently in this situation?

What would someone I admire do in this situation?

What consequences can I accept from the choice I am about to make?

What would be the best choice if I looked at this situation from a third party? Like I were looking from the side.

I CAN'T CHANGE

I heard it said that "People don't change" a lot in my life. I used to believe the same a long time ago. Now every time I hear someone say it, I always answer with: "People change if they want to."

Working on yourself is never easy, but only those who don't want to change will say, "I can't change." They should replace it with "I don't want to change." This is the true statement.

This wall is not as difficult to destroy. Anyone can change if they want to and are ready to do something about it. But if that is not your desire, and someone is pressuring you to change, even if it is for your own good, it will never work.

First of all, it has to be your decision to make a change and your determination to make it all happen.

Stories To Break The Wall

Here I will use the example of addiction. Addictions are usually the most difficult to fight to change yourself and your habits for good.

There is no secret that many now-famous people struggled with addiction or substance abuse in the past (to name just a few: Tim Allen, Angelina Jolie, Drew Barrymore, and Robert Downey, Jr). But if they had not decided to change themselves and turn their lives around, the world might never have known their talents.

I know this is an extreme example. You might need only a minor course correction. Nevertheless, the approach is the same.

How To Crack This Wall

Understand why you need it and if it is truly your choice to change. If someone is begging you to do it, but it is not in your best interest, forget it.

Then understand what good will come from your change. Sit down and write out a list of what will happen in your life and the lives of others as a result of changing.

Now expect that consequences are not always beneficial, even if the change is. Write another list of what not-so-good things might happen so you are prepared for them as well.

To give you an example, if you are determined to change, and you start to make changes to your lifestyle, not everyone in your circle might be happy or comfortable with it. They will start pushing back by saying things like "I don't like who you are becoming, this is not the person I met, I liked you more before"… and so on. Be ready to push through these barriers.

By changing yourself, your life will adjust as well. Some people might change with you, some people will leave on their own, and some will have to be cut out of your life. Don't be scared. It is all part of personal growth.

Ask yourself these questions:

How determined am I to go through this change on a scale from 1 to 10?

If it is not 10, what will make it 10?

Why do I need this change?

What will keep me motivated and committed to this change?

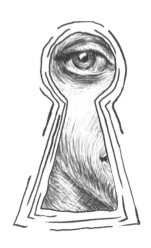

I WAS NOT TAUGHT THE RIGHT WAY

I know we all like to play the victim in any possible situation. It is much easier to put the responsibility on someone else than admit that now you have the power to change it.

I want to tell you a little story about one of my friends. He always says he has no talent for anything. He would love to have a hobby but doesn't know what he could do… because his parents never taught him the right way. His parents never had time for him and didn't take him to any activities such as sports, music, art, or anything else that he could grow up liking or enjoying, at least at the level of having it as a hobby.

If this speaks to you, I have news for you. This is 100% *your* wall, and you need to work on it to free yourself and realize that now you are grown up and can make your own decisions about anything you would like to do or not.

Back to the story: every time I ask this friend, "Why don't you do it now?" he answers… did you guess? "I wasn't taught this way."

Every time my eyes go wide with shock, and I say: "Don't you realize that you don't need your mother or father to do it now? You can do everything you ever wanted to try. It doesn't matter what way you were taught."

This is just one example of when this wall comes up. Below, I will tell my own story from a childhood similar to his but with opposite thinking.

Stories To Break The Wall

My childhood was good. I didn't have everything I wanted, but I had enough. Most importantly, I saw how hard my parents were trying to give me the best they could, so I never complained. I was an active and curious child who wanted to try everything, but often my parents could not afford certain things.

My whole childhood, I wanted roller skates. I watched kids on their roller skates and wished I had some of my own. From time to time, I could borrow a pair for a few minutes a day. I loved every moment. When I was old enough, I think maybe 16 or 17, I worked every summer to make a bit of money. I finally collected enough to buy my own roller skates. After that, I enjoyed them every other evening for several years until, at 19, I started to travel, and I gifted them to my niece.

How To Crack This Wall

You might wonder how this story relates to being taught the right way. Here it is: if you are reading this book, you are most likely old enough to make your own decisions and teach yourself.

So every time you feel like this is the phrase you want to say, bite your tongue and say instead, *Maybe I wasn't taught this (the right) way, but now I can choose how to teach myself the way I want.*

Empower yourself and stop being a victim of the past.

Ask yourself these questions:

What is the right way for me?

What if I had gotten the best my parents had to offer?

What if my parents weren't taught the right way? If they had broken this wall, my life would have been much better. But now it is my time to make a decision about how I want to be taught.

What would I like to do or try that before I couldn't?

I AM A MESS

Sometimes we feel like a mess and maybe even look like one. But the worst is if you call yourself a mess all the time. I have met people who would publicly call themselves stupid or a mess several times a day, somehow expecting to get out of that feeling one day.

In my country, we have a saying: *"Your boat will sail the way you named it."*

Usually, we say this when we label our children or call them a specific nickname over and over again. We also say that if you call your child a pig 100 times, he or she will oink one day...

So, guess what will happen to you if you call yourself a mess? Even if you weren't in fact a mess, you would always feel like one because your brain would believe what you are telling yourself.

And because "being a mess" can have so many different meanings, believe me, the Universe will deliver all of it to you. You will find more and more disorder in your life, including in your career, personal life, finances, health, and so on.

Why It Happens

Some of us play the victim on purpose, unconsciously hoping that people will feel sorry for us in some way. Maybe we would even benefit from it.

Some just think of themselves that way and don't filter their language when they open their mouth to speak.

How To Crack This Wall

I get it. Life gets messy, and we might feel like a mess and look like one, but even then, we must never call ourselves one. Instead, use positive phrases, like: I am working on improving my situation; I am working it out;

I am a work in progress; I am figuring it out; I am planning to fix it; I am working on it; I am just getting started; and so on, whichever suits you best in your specific situation.

Ask yourself these questions:

What words can I use to describe myself or my situation in a more positive way?

What if, just by thinking differently about myself, I could change the way I feel and act?

How often do I think that way?

How will I catch this thought and turn it around?

IT IS TOO LATE FOR ME

From the age I could dream about who I wanted to be—I think I was around five years old—I told my parents I wanted to be a gymnast. Unfortunately, they didn't have time to take me to any classes. But I remember using everything I had available to learn some simple tricks and become more flexible. I remember learning how to do a backbend by walking my hands up and down the wall for several weeks in a row. I had some rings that I could hang in my doorframe, and I remember every minute of my day when I didn't have to do anything else, I would hang and try some tricks. I had no idea of any specific technique; I just tried what my body was capable of. One day, I showed my mother what I had achieved: I made a complete backbend with my wrists touching my heels. I remember my mother and I were impressed by what I had achieved in such a short time. I tried to prove to my parents that I deserved to go to gymnastics and that something could come out of it.

Nothing came of it. Years went by. I think I was about nine or ten, and I still had that dream to be a gymnast. I asked my parents again but was told it was too late for me, that the age to start was five. It made me sad, and I felt like it wasn't fair, but I accepted it because that was what I was told.

Why did I pick this story? Because I have a great story of a lady who didn't think any age was too old, even for something like gymnastics.

When do you think is too late for you? Maybe I could prove you wrong.

Stories To Break The Wall

"Johanna Quaas," according to Wikipedia, "became known worldwide when on March 26th 2012, [a] YouTube user [...] uploaded two videos of the 86-year-old training during the Tournament of Masters in Cottbus, one on the parallel bars and one of a floor exercise routine. The clips became viral videos, and within six days of posting had generated over 1.1 million views each."[7]

You could say no, it is different. Quaas started gymnastics at a young age, and then life happened, and she came back to it when she could because it was her passion. But she didn't retire early as the majority of gymnasts do, and even at 91, she was still active.

So what about now?

When do you think is too late to do something for whatever reason?

How To Crack This Wall

Find other people who do what you would like to do or who started at your age or maybe even later. I am sure you are not alone.

Remember, if some have done it already, you can too. But even if you are the first one, you can prove to others who doubt it is possible.

Ask yourself these questions:

What if I am wrong?

What if it works out just fine? Is it worth a try?

What if I am here to prove it is possible and to break some limits?

Where could I start?

7 "Johanna Quaas." In *Wikipedia*, April 20, 2023. https://en.wikipedia.org/w/index. php?title=Johanna_Quaas&oldid=1150882408.

I AM NOT THAT SPECIAL

I remember being a small girl. I wanted to believe that I was special somehow. And every couple of years, this thought would rise again. I wanted to believe that I had a connection to something bigger or higher than us all, and that I could do things that others couldn't.

It seems that when we are children, we are more likely to know the absolute truth about ourselves. Each of us is special in a unique way. We know we have it in us. We know we have a connection to a greater power. But sometimes, our surroundings build that wall for us, trying to prove us wrong in so many ways.

We start to believe that we are not so special after all, and even when our inner child is trying to tell us the opposite, we silence it and explain to ourselves that it is absolute nonsense. Even if we believed it before, nothing happened. No one saw it, including you. You intuitively felt it, but cannot find proof, so you give up.

It can take decades to remember what is special about you, and it only happens if you are looking. But if you build this wall and never think of the opposite, you will live a lackluster life and die, hopefully remembered by few… or maybe not.

Why It Happens

The world population has reached 8 billion in November 2022.[8] When we come into the world, we care less about how many more people there are, and we are absolutely sure that we came to be special. I wonder if Jesus had that same feeling or if he knew it right away.

Most people never go deep enough to explore their uniqueness and greatness. What for? We are brainwashed by social media and other sources

---

8 Nations, United. "World Population to Reach 8 Billion on 15 November 2022." United Nations. Accessed July 30, 2023. https://www.un.org/en/desa/world-population-reach-8-billion-15-november-2022.

of influence by those unique people who don't feel afraid to look for their uniqueness and are not afraid to be special.

But those regular people made themselves extraordinary by making sacrifices, achieving mastery, and becoming self-aware to find their uniqueness and greatness.

How To Crack This Wall

Decide how you want to be remembered. Material things usually vanish too fast and are never remembered. No one will remember a guy who had the biggest yacht. But people will remember kindness and uniqueness.

Ask yourself these questions:

If I die tomorrow or in a month, what legacy would I leave?

What should others know me for?

What if I am special in some way? What way would that be?

When I was a child, what did I think was special about myself?

I WILL NEVER BE SUCCESSFUL

You are right unless you break this wall.

*"Success usually comes to those who are too busy looking for it."—**Henry David Thoreau***

The craziest thing about success is that it is different for everyone. It is kind of like happiness. When I ask what happiness means for someone specifically, not many people know how to answer. It is the same with success.

The statement "I want to be successful" usually doesn't have an exact meaning attached. But "I will never be successful" has a strong negative energy that supports the entire wall of average.

Most likely, you are terrified to commit to success because failure is unavoidable on this road.

Why It Happens

According to CNBC:

"Success isn't just having lots of money. Many people with lots of money have horribly unhappy and radically imbalanced lives. Success is continuously improving who you are, how you live, how you serve, and how you relate."[9]

Read the above again and again until you finally get it. Success is not just having a lot of money. In fact, just money, the money you didn't work for, which was just granted to you with no purpose, will not make you successful or happy, and in the long run, it could make you even more miserable.

---

9 Hardy, Benjamin. "Why Most People Will Never Be Successful." CNBC, July 14, 2017. https://www.cnbc.com/2017/07/14/why-most-people-will-never-be-successful.html.

You don't have a clear goal to work toward. You get up daily without a specific purpose and action plan. You don't understand what success is to you and how you can grow into it. GROW INTO IT!

How To Crack This Wall

I have to go back to my first book here and mention four ways to invest in yourself: Body, Mind, Spirit, and Relationships. This is where everything starts. Spend your days with high-quality activities. You must focus on what is important and what matters not only to you but to others and find your own meaning of success. Remember, material things barely mean anything… it just means more sh*t to clean up or sell after you die.

Ask yourself these questions:

What legacy would I leave if I died tomorrow or in a month?

What is success, not looking at others but looking deep inside?

Why do I want it?

What will I do with it?

After all, not everyone wants to be successful, and that is okay too, if you accept it.

I AM NOT GOOD WITH MONEY/ I WILL ALWAYS BE BROKE

We do have a lot of money walls that were built by society, including by our parents or caregivers. But I am impressed by a new generation of workers and their ways of thinking about how they can make money out of thin air, almost literally. There are several things I learned from 25-year-olds who had a similar background to mine. They arrived in a foreign country with nothing but one piece of luggage and no money, and in only a few years were making more than $100K annually, not working particularly hard and not even knowing the language. And some creative young people even earn a million dollars a year, without overthinking it much at all!

Now, guess what? The thought of not being good with money or being broke never visited their minds. They didn't even think for a second that was an option.

Why It Happens

"Many people take no care of their money till they come nearly to the end of it, and others do just the same with their time."—**Johann Wolfgang von Goethe**

Our limits are exactly what we think they are. So if you think, I will always be broke, you will feel broke and act accordingly. There will be no surprise: you will not just wake up one day suddenly good with money. It is just not going to happen unless you adopt a different belief and feeling about your relationship with money.

I know that sometimes the story we were told for years by our parents and other people around us seems to be true. And you may wonder, Who am I to change history or stand out by thinking differently?

How To Crack This Wall

Read "I Will Never Make More Than." There are several tools that can be used here as well.

But another one is to make a list of why you can be trusted with money.

Then find your current beliefs and forgive everyone who is involved in them.

Breathe deeply and let it go.

Ask yourself these questions:

What qualities do I have that make me good with money?

What limiting beliefs do I have now about money?

With what new beliefs can I replace them?

Why am I holding on to my current beliefs? Are they even true?

49

I DO NOT HAVE THE RIGHT COMPLEXION OR BODY TYPE

Have you ever looked in the mirror and told yourself that you can't do certain things because of your skin color, body weight, hair color, or something else?

If you are lucky to have a perfect appearance that works for everything, and your parents always told you that you were perfect in everything you did, you have developed absolute confidence.

But more likely, you find flaws in the way you look. Other people influence how we feel about our appearance.

I will tell you about my body conflict. I have always loved to dance. When I was in a dance group, I felt discriminated against because I was tall. The rest of the dance group wasn't, and I guess aesthetically, I didn't look right dancing with them, even in the back row.

Most of the time, if the group traveled, I wasn't invited because I didn't fit in. I could be called at the last minute to replace someone who got sick, for example, and most of the time, I was placed in the very back due to being taller than everyone else. The worst part was that my technique and my performance were better than some among the traveling group.

Right there, if I had believed I was too tall to dance, I would have quit and never returned. Instead, what did I think? That they weren't the right group for me, or that I was not in the right place to show my talent.

With that, I kept going and became a teacher and choreographer. That way, no one could tell me what size and what height I had to be… it didn't matter anymore. In case you are wondering, my career in this field lasted about five years, but I still dance and sometimes teach classes.

Stories To Break The Wall

Tess Holliday, according to Wikipedia, is:

"[…] an American plus-size model, blogger, and makeup artist. At the age of 15, while she was a US size 16 (UK 18/20) and 5 feet 3 inches tall, Holliday auditioned at a casting call for plus models in Atlanta, Georgia, where she was told she would be lucky to do print advertisements or catalogue work because she was too short and big."[10]

If she had believed these remarks the first time around, she probably would be living a miserable life. But Holliday became a professional model in 2011 while working as a Los Angeles dental office receptionist. And now she is famous, does what she loves the most, loves her body, and encourages others to do the same.

How To Crack This Wall

Understand if someone criticizes you about your appearance and says that you can't do something because of that… it doesn't mean anything. Besides, this specific person didn't like you. But there are a lot of others who would. You just need to find the right place and the right audience. Or create it for yourself, as Holliday did.

Don't obsess over other people's opinions of you.

Find your passion, and don't be afraid to follow it, even if you are not the right fit. You can shape the world to make yourself a right fit.

Ask yourself these questions:

What makes me believe I don't fit this job/role/passion?

What should I believe to make it work?

How can I find the right place if I don't fit in here?

---

10 "Tess Holliday." In *Wikipedia*, July 25, 2023. https://en.wikipedia.org/w/index.php?title=Tess_Holliday&oldid=1167017381.

I HAVE A LOT OF PROBLEMS

"Problems are the gifts that make us dig out and figure out who we are, what we're made for, and what we're responsible to give back to life."— **Tony Robbins**

You might be going through difficulties. It is part of life. To understand good, we need to dip into bad. To be born again, nature dies first. All life consists of waves or swings. Did you swing to negative? You will go back to positive, as long as you don't build your wall of no return—because if you do, you will hit the wall every time you try to swing back.

Problems do happen, and every problem has a solution. If it doesn't, there are two ways to look at it: it is not your problem to solve, or if you can't do anything about it, then there is nothing to be done... I know it might sound weird, but you just need to live through the experience and try to look for the positive side to it. Often there is one, but we are so concentrated on the negative that we can't see past it. The problem gets so big in our eyes that we can't step past it to see what is next.

This wall will only lock all your problems inside and might bring other problems in, but nothing will go out. So the more you say it or think it, the more it will become true. It will confirm your idea of life and the collection of issues in it.

Why It Happens

I hope you believe that our thinking creates our reality, and it is energy on its own that will impact you and others around you. If you did not believe that or at least admit that it could be true, you wouldn't be holding this book.

Do you feel sorry for yourself? Do you want others to feel sorry for you? Do you believe that your problems will never end and that this is your life?

Talking about problems and negative things is addictive, releasing a chemical in our brain that we unconsciously crave. Without realizing it, we become masochists, continuing to fill the need for that chemical release to our brain once again.

Some people will spend all their time poisoning themselves by bringing more pain into their lives. And what can be created from that? Nothing but a disease that will eat your body from the inside.

It is time to break the cycle.

How To Crack This Wall

Ask yourself, **Why am I facing this problem? What is it showing me? Where do I need to pay more attention?**

Find the positive side to it. I assure you it is there. The Creator has a bigger picture. **What do I need to learn from it? By developing a solution, will it make me grow?**

Address one problem at a time and then move to the next one. Stop complaining and feeling sorry for yourself. I promise you are not alone. Other people in the world are dealing with the same things. It is up to you how you will get out. Be stronger, or give up.

I CAN'T HAVE EVERYTHING I WANT

The thing is, we don't need to have it all. It would be overwhelming. You just need what you need and what was meant for you and you only.

You see, everything takes place at the right time. You may not have what you want now, but the future comes with open doors and possibilities. And if one day it comes to you, then it was meant for you, but if it doesn't, then someone has a bigger picture, and what you want is not what you need. Keep on working and keep on wanting.

The statement might be true, but a wall like that will stop you from dreaming and wanting more in your life.

Why It Happens

Your past has an effect on your confidence. It could be your parents who liked to tell you as a child, "You can't have everything you want," maybe when you saw that scooter or bike you wanted so bad. Your past probably instilled some doubt in your possibilities, and now you just say it to yourself as an excuse. The excuse will keep you low enough to not want anything.

Everything we gain in our life and become proud of usually begins with our wants and wishes. We want to have a home, we want to have kids, and we want to have a successful career and a healthy marriage. Once we have "it," we are proud of it. But if it didn't begin with a want, it would not begin at all.

How To Crack This Wall

Change your belief and rephrase. Instead of building and supporting the wall of IMPOSSIBLE, make it the road of POSSIBLE.

You can start by saying something like:

I can have everything I need and that was meant for me.

Then it is up to you to believe what is meant for you and how you can get there.

Ask yourself these questions:

What do I think I want but can't have?

What makes me think I can't have it?

Why do I need it?

What will change if I change the way I think about it?

"Whatever we plant in our subconscious mind and nourish with repetition and emotion will one day become a reality."—***Earl Nightingale***

I AM NOT LUCKY

I used to believe the same about myself. I used to work 10 times harder and still would not get the desired result. But a friend of mine, on the other hand, didn't put any effort into anything, and everything would just flow to her every time she said it or wished for it. I used to think she was just lucky, and I wasn't. I would say, *I am just not lucky and have to work ten times harder to make anything come my way.* So, I unconsciously created a double wall in my mind that would keep me working hard and still not getting any results.

I have the craziest story that turned this around and broke my wall, which I will tell you about later. But after I realized what had changed and what had been holding me back all these years, a light went on in my head. I thought it was much easier than the path I took to turn this thing around.

What is luck? And why do we think that some have it and some don't? What influences so-called luck? And how can you start attracting it into your life without voodoo spells or shamanic rituals?

Why It Happens

You, like me, probably saw someone who had an easier way to get something and believed that they were just luckier than you. Then you went on thinking that you were not fortunate and that it was just the way it is. Some lucky people will get everything they want, but definitely not you.

What if I told you that lucky, or not, is in your head only, and that your thoughts and beliefs decide how lucky you will be next time?

It is from the category: *"Whether you think you can or think you can't, you're right."—Henry Ford*

How To Crack This Wall

Start believing you are lucky *now*. How? This is how my story went…

At 21 years old, I was tired of being unlucky and working ten times harder than others. So I decided to get a tattoo with the Japanese characters for luck, abundance, and something else... I can't remember the last one anymore. I did get the tattoo, and after that, everything changed almost overnight. Things started to come my way much easier.

Hold on a minute—I am not telling you to get a tattoo to turn your luck around. My tattoo became like a talisman, making me believe that I was lucky and that there was no way around it. But I did tattoo it on my body. You don't have to. The same goes for those talismans that bring luck to us in one way or another. But in reality, with our talismans, we act a different way—more confident, more competent, and, I guess, LUCKIER.

So if you need a talisman to believe that you are the lucky one, why not? Get something: a crocodile leg, a frog eye, red string, or, in my case, a tattoo... But the best lucky charm is the belief that from now on, you are the lucky one around here.

You can start by saying something like:

I am luckier than I thought before.

Ask yourself these questions:

What makes me think that lucky person didn't work hard for it?

How can I change my beliefs about luck?

What would make me lucky?

PART II:
They Walls

"A man is but the product of his thoughts. What he thinks, he becomes."—**Mahatma Gandhi**

As you understand already, "I Walls" are the walls you think about yourself. "They Walls" are what you think of others or what you think people think of you.

It might be confusing, but we often depend on someone else's opinion, and we even make up what other people might think of us, which most likely is not true, but we will get to this later.

Our mind tricks us sometimes into believing that we know what other people think, especially when there are gaps in our understanding and we need to fill them with something. You can be talking to a person, then someone asks you an uncomfortable question, or maybe the person is out of your comfort zone. You answer, and seconds later, you think, I should not have said that, they probably think I'm stupid or something else like that. And that is just the beginning. Then you get a tsunami of thoughts about what the other person might think of you.

Read very carefully here: not many people listen attentively to what you have to say. While you answer their question, most are thinking about where to go for dinner, or they remembered something from work. Very few will intentionally listen and even fewer will think something negative about you.

So in this part, we will talk about what those limiting thoughts are and how they influence everything we do. We will follow the same pattern and will look into why it happens and how to crack those walls.

But before you start, I want to challenge you to think of one belief that you have about other people and what they think of you.

Write it down, and if you don't find it here, email it to me at info@ambitiouswe.com. I am curious to know what you have on your mind and what I missed.

Let's dive in and see if you find your wall and ways to break it.

PEOPLE DON'T LIKE ME

How did you determine this? Maybe you feel a bit different from others, and a few people in one place said something that wasn't nice to hear. And that is when you decided that all people, almost everyone you interact with, don't like you. Why would they? You probably find a good explanation for that one too, something like, *I am an extrovert, I'm bad at holding a simple conversation, I'm a freak, I don't belong in this world*, and so on.

Now, anywhere you go, before you see someone who enjoys your company, you will find a few who don't, not because it is true but because your brain concentrates on proving that you are right. Your mind is looking for any potential hook to show you that your thoughts are correct.

Why It Happens

Remember the first time in your life when you thought this phrase to yourself. What was the situation, and what happened? At one point, did you build that wall? You could be looking at some accumulated trauma from your childhood. Someone may have repeated to you some stupid things. But this message wasn't yours to begin with. They piled their issues and traumas onto you. You didn't know how to protect yourself emotionally at that time, and you sucked it in like a sponge. Now the impression of someone not liking you is following you around like a ghost.

Another reason, and this one could be big as well, is that you don't like yourself, or you hate something about yourself. You can't forgive yourself for something. Because you cannot, you think others won't either.

How To Crack This Wall

First of all, and you probably read it in this book already, forgive. Forgive yourself and forgive anyone who might do this to you. I know forgiveness is not easy, and for some of us it must be done every time we face a situation or a person again. But forgiveness is done not for them, but for you, so you can let the sorrow go and move forward with an open heart.

I finished a book three months ago, and I am still thinking about what I read. The name of the book is *The Untethered Soul* by Michael A. Singer. In it, he says anytime you go through an unpleasant situation or negative emotions, relax your heart and let it pass through you. Otherwise, every time you close yourself, you lock that energy inside, and it will keep bothering you and eating at you from the inside.

So, what if you let that go, start fresh with an open mind and heart, and see if you find someone who will like you? Once you start to see, you can't unsee, and you will meet more and more people who do like you.

You can start by saying something like:

I am liked by others. People love me.

Ask yourself these questions:

What is likable about me?

What makes me not like myself?

What will make me forgive myself and others?

How can I find someone who likes me?

PEOPLE DON'T CHANGE

You are probably correct about this one, but hear me out. I used to think the same, and I saw a great example of it. Just don't tell my husband; he might be jealous or happy...

My first boyfriend, whom I dated for years, proposed to me, and I said NO. My mom was in shock. We dated for five years, and my entire family treated him as my future husband. He loved me like nothing else in his life. Why did I say NO? When my mom asked me, my answer was that: people don't change. I heard him talking to his mom on the phone, rude and angry every time she called. I knew one day he would speak to me that way too.

I will never know if I was right, but I am glad it happened the way it did, and I have no regrets about my past life, as it brought me where I am right now, doing what I love. And again, I think it is one of the walls that was raised high during my childhood.

But now I know better! And every time I hear someone say, "People don't change," my response now is different. People do change if they want to and are determined about it.

Here is the catch: you cannot change anyone else. It doesn't matter how hard you try. But you can change yourself if you genuinely want to and are ready to put up the fight with the present version of yourself and keep the fight up when the past dark version appears in front of you once again.

Stories To Break The Wall

According to *The Muse*:

"Tyler Perry had a rough childhood. He was physically and sexually abused growing up, got kicked out of high school, and tried to commit suicide twice—once as a preteen and again at 22. At 23, he moved to Atlanta and took up odd jobs as he started working on his stage career. In fact, Perry was named Forbes' highest paid man in entertainment in 2011."[11]

In 2022, his net worth was $1 billion. Given his childhood, Perry's story might have turned out very differently. But at one point, something clicked. He changed the way he thought and never gave up on getting where he wanted to be.

How To Crack This Wall

Ask yourself these questions:

Why do I think this is true?

Whom do I know personally or not who changed tremendously for the better?

Could I change if I really wanted to?

Who am I trying to change into?

Realize one thing: you can't change anyone but yourself. You can do something to influence others' decisions to change by showing what is possible and the benefits of that change.

You can start by saying something like:***People DO change, if they are ready and willing to fight for it.***

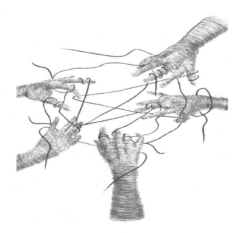

11 The Muse. "9 Famous People Who Will Inspire You to Never Give Up," March 27, 2014. https://www.themuse.com/advice/9-famous-people-who-will-inspire-you-to-never-give-up.

PEOPLE WILL JUDGE ME

When was the last time you absolutely froze before doing something important or something you enjoy just from thinking about what people would say about you or how they would judge you?

It is one of the reasons many people are afraid of public speaking. We are so scared to make a fool of ourselves, afraid of what they will think and what they will say about our failure.

Did you know that mistakes are fundamental to our learning? As we try new things and push the boundaries to get where we want to be, errors are unavoidable. Stopping because you are too preoccupied with what other people will think is absurd.

There are 100 opinions from 100 people, and there are always people who won't like you. It doesn't matter what you do or how you do it. Don't be afraid to be judged, be afraid from being prevented from doing what makes you happy, what drives your passion. Remember, people who judge are not to be worried about because they don't have their own thing going on and have too much time to stick their nose in someone else's business. People who are successful with their own life and growth will be supportive and respectful, and they will definitely understand what it takes to achieve your goals, even if you make mistakes on the way up.

You might have read it in my previous book, but I will say it here once again:

Every single human was brought to this planet with some specific mission or assignment. We are all looking for it, and we call it a career. Some people get lucky and know from a young age what they are meant to do. But for most of us, it takes decades, and some people ask themselves that question before they die without fulfilling their purpose.

So don't be the last just because you are afraid to be judged by others.

Why It Happens

We are part of a community, and since our childhood, we looked for the approval of our parents. The good part about it is that we learned what was safe, and we learned important life skills. But sometimes, the thought grows bigger than it needs to be to serve us, and we start to look for the approval of everyone around us, whether it is from our friends, our loved ones, or any person we meet (or don't—social media sometimes says a lot).

How To Crack This Wall

If you are determined to be successful in your own way, people will judge you, but it should not be a wall in your mind that stops you or slows you down.

You can start by saying something like:

Judgement is not a reason for me to stop or slow down on the way to my success.

Ask yourself these questions:

How is judgement affecting me now?

What do I need to think to not pay attention to judgement?

69

What if judgement helped me to push through and grow?

What can judgement help me with?

PEOPLE WON'T UNDERSTAND ME

This wall stands so close to the previous one. You might have built them together, or you might have only one of them. But what I know for sure is that this wall gives us headaches and a whole bunch of overthinking when it is not needed at all, to the point of losing sleep over it.

It took me some time to stop worrying about what other people think of me or my situation. I only take what I know they told me as truth, and I make sure I understood it right. I remember it is just their opinion, and if it is not true to me and what I am trying to do, it doesn't mean anything and should not keep my attention for too long.

The most talented people and geniuses in this world weren't understood by others around them, especially by their families. Not everyone needs to understand you. They might not know what you do.

Stories To Break The Wall

*"Why is it that nobody understands me, yet everybody likes me?"—**Albert Einstein***

According to Walter Isaacson:

"Being taunted on his walks to and from school based on 'racial characteristics about which the children were strangely aware' helped reinforce the sense of being an outsider, which would stay with Einstein his entire life."[12]

Einstein is known for his theory of relativity, which at the time seemed like total nonsense to the scientific community, but he has many more genius achievements and discoveries to his name. And for sure, that picture of him with crazy hair.

---

12 Isaacson, Walter. *Einstein: His Life and Universe.* New York: Simon & Schuster, 2007.

How To Crack This Wall

Remember, those who need to *will* understand you, if not now, then eventually. Some people get recognized only after they leave this mortal world. Of course, it doesn't mean you need to live your whole life misunderstood. I say this amazing phrase to myself all the time: *You will not know until you try, and it is better to try and know you gave it a chance than to not try and always wonder "What if?"*

You can start by saying something like:

Not everyone needs to understand me or what I am doing. It might come to them later in their lives.

Ask yourself these questions:

What makes me want people to understand me?

What do they need to understand?

What if I could communicate it better? How would it sound?

THEY THINK IT COMES EASY TO ME

Everyone thinks you are just lucky and that everything comes to you like manna from the sky. They believe everything you have accomplished so far and everything you are doing now is effortless. Sound familiar? Or they might not know how difficult it was for you to get where you are. What do you hope to gain from their understanding of how much work you put in?

"Why is this thought a wall?" you might ask.

When people don't see all your hard work, and they just see the results, this wall will stop you from putting all the effort needed into reaching your full potential.

You know, we look at famous people and think they have it so easy and that someone does the work for them. But the truth is that we don't know a big chunk of their story and what they went through.

I just finished reading *Can't Hurt Me* by David Goggins. If you knew him before as an athlete, you probably thought he was made for that and was running from the time he was born. But when you read his story, you realize how much effort he put into everything he did, including losing 100 pounds just for a chance to qualify for Navy Seal training.

We tend to focus on results and usually don't see all the work that was done before. We only know the truth of our own sacrifice, how we pushed our limits, and how hard it was.

Why It Happens

Only in the last few decades has it become popular to reveal our backstories and what it took for some of us, not just famous people, to get where we are today. It wasn't talked about, making so many think that success is effortless. Only now do we start to open our minds to the idea that everyone started at zero and, most likely, the road to success wasn't easy for anyone.

It wasn't your success if it was delivered to you on a silver platter.

How To Crack This Wall

The good thing is that if people see your success, that means you mastered something that now seems effortless from the outside, and you will inspire others to try the same.

It is not time to quit just because no one sees how much you already did.

Rather, it is the perfect time to tell people your story. Tell your friends and others around you. I am sure they will appreciate your openness and can learn a thing or two from you.

Ask yourself these questions:

What story can I share?

What is important for them to know to understand me better?

Why is it important to me?

THEY KNOW BETTER

Sometimes we fall into the pit by following someone who seems more knowledgeable than us or who, by the nature of their job title, is supposed to know what they are doing. We blindly trust their decisions and their knowledge without doing our homework on whether it is true and if it really works or is good for us.

Recently I saw this in one of my classes. It is not my original idea, but it was eye-opening for me.

Imagine that all the knowledge in the world accumulated by all living and lived beings is a circle. Out of that circle, what is personal knowledge? You probably guessed right: just a little speck, a little tiny dot. One that can't even be seen with the naked eye.

But I will do you a favor and blow it up so you can see. Then your knowledge is what you know you know and what you know what you don't know.

And the rest of that universe's knowledge is what you don't know that you don't know. Outside of that circle is what no one knows.

As you can see, those you look up to don't know everything either. They might know more than you, and you need to learn from them, but don't forget to do your homework and don't underestimate yourself. Because the cool thing about knowledge is that it is available to everyone.

Why It Happens

We often have two opposing thoughts: we either think we don't know and can't learn it, or we know everything and only our truth is the right one. But neither of those is correct in any way.

How To Crack This Wall

I know one thing for sure: no one knows better what is best for you. This is only for you to figure out. So don't be afraid to step out of your comfort zone and learn something new. Prove to yourself that the only person who knows what is best for you is you, but only in your healthy state of mind.

You can start by saying something like:

They might know more, but I know what is better for me.

Ask yourself these questions:

What is this wall stopping me from?

What am I afraid of?

Where am I giving away my power again?

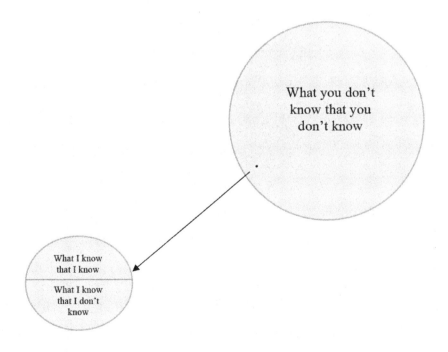

THEY DON'T KNOW MY PAST

You know, you are absolutely right. No one knows your past as well as you. But our past doesn't define who we can become tomorrow if we are ready to take control of our present. We are the product of our past, but more often than not, your past shaped your current state and personality to serve you in your future.

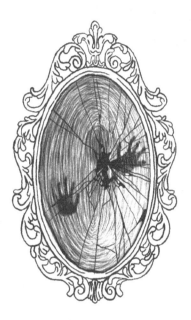

It is not them who is holding you back with this wall, but it is you who can't let go of your past and start working on your present to get the future that you want.

Our past can be complicated in many ways, but you must learn to find your strength, not pity yourself.

"They Walls" are tricky because they are the same as "I Walls." But in I walls, you hold the power and your walls from the inside. With "They Walls," you think it is other people holding your walls from the outside, but when you finally break through one, you realize that everyone has your face.

The faster you uncover these truths, the faster you can regain power and destroy your walls.

Why It Happens

When life gets hard, we like to blame our past and think if only it had been perfect, or just normal, then it would be so much easier today. But an easy past doesn't make a strong person. So you might need to rewrite your story from a different perspective: the perspective of what that past brought you and how it shaped you for the challenges you are facing today.

My father wasn't a great father. I am grateful for everything he did give me, like my education. But I am even more grateful for everything he didn't give me because it taught me how to make my own decisions, care for myself from a young age, and make my own money.

This is how I tell myself my story about my father. He taught me lessons without knowing them himself.

How To Crack This Wall

We often concentrate on the negative, and switching to a positive radar is difficult. But once you start to see even something small from a positive perspective, it will become easier and easier.

You have to make a point of taking time out of your day to sit down and think hard about what is positive there. Don't start your list with negative stuff; try hard to find one or a few positive outcomes.

You can also tell your story to others and share the lesson you learned.

Ask yourself these questions:

What are those positive outcomes that I have from a negative past?

Why is my past holding me back?

What one thought do I need to change to make my future brighter?

What is the lesson I learned?

THEY DON'T SEE MY POTENTIAL

This wall will definitely make you give up on your dream, especially if you know you can do more and you have something unique to offer the world. I know how it feels. This was my wall when I worked for a company as Customer Assistant Specialist (simply put, Receptionist). I knew I could do more and better. And when I finally applied within the company for a higher position, I got turned down because they didn't feel like I would stay long enough at the position.

So I took a leap of faith. I left the company and looked for what I deserved at a different one. And it worked. When I left the company, someone else gave me a chance and hired me, and that is where I bloomed like a flower and showed my beautiful petals of ambition, potential, and organization.

I know this wall seems big enough to stop you from taking your path to success. But sometimes, you can walk right around it and get someone else to believe in you and see your potential.

This is the time for some inspiring self-talk. Tell yourself that you know what is meant for you and that you know you will get there, and if people in front of you don't see it, turn to the side and shine your potential to others. Or keep proving yourself till you get through the wall.

Stories To Break The Wall

We all remember the old movie *Rocky*, which was so popular and even has its own statue in Philadelphia. But it wasn't easy for Sylvester Stallone. According to *Forbes*:

"In the early 70s, Stallone was an unknown actor trying to make it in New York. He had minor success in the movie *The Lords Of Flatbush* but was still broke.

"'After *The Lords Of Flatbush*, I decided it was time to come to California, so I moved to California and things weren't going so well there. As a matter a fact, I actually had to go out and try to sell my dog because it was either that or he wasn't going to be very well fed around the house,' said Stallone in an interview with Michael Watson."[13]

He wrote a script and wanted to have the main role. One production company offered him $360,000 for the script, with the condition that he wouldn't play Rocky. Remember that he had no car, $106 in the bank, and sold his dog for $50 to pay the bills.

They didn't see his potential to play this role. They liked the script but not Sylvester Stallone as an actor. He actually took a cut for his script just to get the role. And this was his best decision. *Rocky* received nine Oscar nominations and got three wins, including Best Picture, and grossed over $200 million. (By the way, he bought his dog back for $3,000.)

In 2023, Sylvester Stallone is an actor, screenwriter, producer, and director who has a net worth of $400 million.

13 Ward, Tom. "The Amazing Story Of The Making Of 'Rocky.'" Forbes. Accessed July 30, 2023. https://www.forbes.com/sites/tomward/2017/08/29/the-amazing-story-of-the-making-of-rocky/.

How To Crack This Wall

Sometimes the main person who needs to see your potential is you because if you know that you were meant for more, that is enough to keep trying to prove to others that you can do it, even if the road to success is not as you first expected.

You can start by saying something like:

I know I am meant for more, and I believe in myself.

Ask yourself these questions:

What could be my next step to find someone who believes in me?

What do I think my future looks like?

Who do I think might believe in me?

SOMEONE WILL SAVE ME

So many of us hope that one day someone will come and save us from everything that is going on around or within us.

The Buddha said it so perfectly: "No one saves us but ourselves. No one can, and no one may. We ourselves must walk the path."

Growing up in my country, we still held traditional beliefs, such as all a woman needed in order to do well in life was to marry successfully. It might have changed in recent years, but so many countries are still the same. The problem with this is the wall of someone coming to save you, and there is nothing that depends on you.

Now here is the trick: if you are a strong believer, you will probably disagree here and say we are already saved, and there is nothing we need to do to receive this gift. I am not here to disagree with this but to look on the side of the work that needs to be done by you and no one else.

Proverbs 14:23 TPT says, *"If you work hard at what you do, great abundance will come to you. But merely talking about getting rich while living to only pursue your pleasures brings you face-to-face with poverty."*

I mean that you need to use your talents the best way you can and not expect someone to come and do the work for you.

I think I will stop talking about any religious beliefs. It doesn't matter what religion you consult because they all say similar things.

Don't wait for someone to save you. Save yourself first.

Why It Happens

Only wise people admit their mistakes and take responsibility for what is happening in their lives. We love to blame others for our mistakes, and the same goes for fixing them: we hope that someone else will resolve them for us.

Only people not afraid to take responsibility for their lives may become truly successful and prosper in their own way.

How To Crack This Wall

You can start by saying something like:

I am in control of my life, and I can choose for myself what is right.

This is a hard one to break. If you rely on someone for a long time, you have to break your thinking patterns. It is possible. You need to become conscious of your thoughts, and every time you feel like blaming someone else, find and admit your own choices that led you to where you are now. Then, whenever you hope for someone else to fix your issue, ask yourself what you can do on your own to do your best work or resolve your issue.

Ask yourself these questions:

How did my own choices lead me to where I am right now?

What talents do I need to use to deliver my best work?

Which of my choices needs to be looked at and changed for the future?

Where is my power? What do I do best?

THEY DON'T LET ME/THEY HAVE CONTROL OF ME

This type of wall may be built in two different ways, and they are absolutely opposite.

If you think this way about colleagues, friends, and other people around you, you most likely need to work on your confidence. Like the rest of the "They Walls," you gave all your power away for some reason deep inside. It might be influenced by your past, but it is never too late to start unloading your backpack of bricks before you aren't able to carry it anymore on your shoulders, and one day it could break you. The worst part about this backpack of bricks is that we might pass it to our children unintentionally.

The other type is—and I hate if this is the case and I have to bring this realization to you—if you think that way at home with your partner, or someone who lives with you in the same household, you might be living with abuse or domestic violence. You might not understand, and you are trying to survive by giving all your power away to that person. I am sorry if that is happening to you. There is help out there. Be brave and ask for it.

Why It Happens

I talked so much about giving your power away, and you can use tools from other chapters to start destroying this wall if it is related to you from the side of work or friends. I want to touch a little more on abuse because it happens more often than we know and talk about it.

According to the National Institutes of Health:

"Domestic violence is a common problem in the United States, affecting an estimated 10 million people every year; as many as one in four women and one in nine men are victims of domestic violence. Domestic and family violence includes economic, physical, sexual, emotional, and psychological abuse of children, adults, or elders. Domestic violence causes worsened psychological and physical health, decreased quality of life, decreased productivity, and in some cases, mortality."[14]

It is much more challenging to recognize emotional or psychological abuse. This form does not leave obvious marks or traces but affects quality of life, causes severe depression, and has destructive effects. And most perpetrators and victims do not seek help. According to *Psych Central*:

"Emotional abuse involves a broad range of tactics, including shaming and gaslighting, which are meant to leave you feeling powerless and hopeless. Depending on the types of emotional abuse and how long you've been dealing with these behaviors, you might experience different effects on your emotional, physical, and mental health. Effects could be low self-esteem, doubt, shame, isolation, loneliness, and many more."[15]

How To Crack This Wall

The best way is to recognize and acknowledge unhealthy relationships and abusive personalities. It is often tough to break the connections between abuser and victim. You will not be able to change that person unless they understand it and seek help independently. But seeking help and trying to leave the abuser would be the best exit from an unhealthy situation.

You can encourage yourself by saying something like:

I am enough!

Ask yourself these questions:

What usually do I hear about myself in the presence of this person?

How often do I hear encouragement and approval?

How do I feel about myself?

How do I want to feel?

---

14 Huecker, Martin R., Kevin C. King, Gary A. Jordan, and William Smock. "Domestic Violence." In *StatPearls*. Treasure Island (FL): StatPearls Publishing, 2023. http://www.ncbi.nlm.nih.gov/books/NBK499891/.
15 Psych Central. "Effects of Emotional Abuse on Your Brain, Relationships, and Health," March 23, 2022. https://psychcentral.com/health/effects-of-emotional-abuse.

THEY WILL BE JEALOUS

Marcus Aurelius once wrote: *"It never ceases to amaze me: we all love ourselves more than other people but care more about their opinion than our own."*

This is the worst reason not to start something you wish or do something you like. Personal growth in any way is possible. You will always face people who are critical, jealous, and resistant to your changes. But if that is something that could stop you from doing what you want and being who you want to be, you probably should not even begin in the first place.

Because any time you start doing something different from what you are used to, you will make some people dislike you in some way or another. And most of the time, the reason is not you but them. You make them feel uncomfortable next to you because you are one step ahead.

If you really look into any famous person's life, they probably have as many haters and jealous people as they have followers.

My story is not any different. Even though I am not that popular yet, I am just working on it. When I started to write my first book, the first resistance I met was from people closest to me, which I had never expected. I always thought they were supposed to support you in all your endeavors, not judge you and try to talk you out of it with some stupid reasoning.

Change is difficult, not just for you but for everyone in your circle, whether friends or family. But so often, we fall into the trap of thinking that maybe they are right and that we should not do anything but stay where we are and within what we already know.

Stories To Break The Wall

Here is my little story about this wall. I was working on my first book and was very excited about anything I created, putting a lot of energy and passion into it. The time for the cover art finally came. I first asked one graphic designer to make one for me, but it was not what I was looking for. So I decided to create a few drafts myself and then pass them to the designer to follow. I wanted it to stay within my idea because it spoke to my identity and story. I had three designs, and it wasn't easy to pick one. So I decided to ask a group of women who come from my country or are close to it. A few just did what was asked and picked their favorites out of three, but a handful of others criticized me in every way possible, even my appearance in the photo I used… like my nose wasn't good enough to have my own photo on the cover of the book I wrote. A few critics were interesting to read to see if there was anything I could do to improve what I already had. But the rest was out of jealousy and resistance.

I am glad I have a good filter to understand what is unimportant and does not apply to me but to their own problems and issues. So I went with the cover image I fell in love with the most. It might not be perfect, but it is what speaks from my heart about my story. I am glad I did. I received so many compliments on how bright it is, and it genuinely reflects me.

How To Crack This Wall

*"INSECURITY breeds JEALOUSY / JEALOUSY creates ENVY / ENVY causes self-destruction / a hater is made up of all three. Just remember you are an opportunity away from being hated on yourself!"— **Carlos Wallace***

I hope this speaks to you. People who are jealous around you are just insecure about themselves.

That is it! That is what you need to remember. It is not your problem, but theirs. All you need to do is to put your pink shades on and do what is in your plan for your personal success.

You can begin by saying something like:

They are jealous because I am going where they wish to be one day, and I can do this.

Ask yourself these questions:

Why should it bother me?

What do I feel in this situation?

What can help me to move forward?

How can I limit unneeded criticism?

By the way, in the end, I just asked Facebook not to send me a notification on the post about any comments. That was all I needed to do to not worry anymore.

THEY DON'T KNOW WHAT I'VE GONE THROUGH

No one knows what you have gone through in your life and how difficult it was. You might have had sleepless nights, painful experiences, and many more challenges to overcome.

But is this the story you keep telling yourself about why you can't do something or why you are not enough?

Yesterday I heard on the radio about a boy who was born with no legs and still successfully played basketball at his school. I hope he will keep his approach to life to inspire others. He chose a different story to tell himself, and it is not a story of a boy with no legs who would never be able to play any sports, hoping people would understand and feel pity for him.

People might feel sorry for you and try to understand, but they can't change the story you keep telling yourself. It is up to you to turn any story, even a bad one, into a strength.

If they did know, what would it change?

Nowadays, it is not that easy to find empathy. If you do, you are lucky. Empathy helps a lot, but your story will stay with you. So it is in your best interest to start transforming your story to draw passion, mission, and much more from it, instead of pain and remorse.

Why It Happens

It is very close to a few other walls we have already discussed. Look for more tools in "They Don't Know My Past" and "They Think It Comes Easy To Me."

I know we are all looking for understanding and empathy, but we are self-centered creatures fighting our own battles. Go to your best friend or family to seek understanding and support in a difficult time, or find the right community to do the same. But use this time productively to change the story you keep telling yourself.

How To Crack This Wall

This amazing exercise will help you look a little bit deeper.

Concentrate one day on the thoughts you tell yourself in specific situations, especially when something goes wrong. The best is if you write them down.

For example, you were five minutes late to pick up your child from school, and you tell yourself just in your mind that you are a bad mom. Or you look at someone skinnier than you, and you say, "I will always be fat," or "That is never going to be me." We say many of those things to ourselves throughout the day without knowing the damage they cause.

You can turn your self-talk in a more positive way by saying something like:

I am doing my best today as a mom.

I am working on myself to be fit.

Use more questions from the chapters I mentioned above.

THEY'VE ALREADY DONE IT/HAVE IT

How often do we stop before we even start just by thinking, What if someone already has it or does it? Someone has surely already invented it or talked about it.

Honestly, I had to scroll back to other walls and check if I didn't tell you this before because it seemed like I had already talked about it so many times, or maybe it was to someone else…

Or maybe someone else already talked to you about this, so there is no reason for me to do it once again… Do you get where I am going with this?

I am sure a lot of things from this book were mentioned by someone else before. I probably didn't invent anything new here, but I am sure thousands more people are talking about it now and will talk about it in the future. There is no need to be the first one.

The crazy thing is that a lot of similar ideas come to many people, sometimes even at the same time. Only a few decide to do something with their idea. So you do have a choice to be one of those few.

Stories To Break The Wall

Here is a history lesson: do you know who invented the telephone? If you do, you probably answered Alexander Graham Bell in 1875. Rumor has it that he wasn't the first who did, and most likely not the only one either. According to *All That's Interesting*:

"Several inventors worked on a similar project at the same time. Elisha Gray was one of them, and the story says that his lawyer made it to the Patent Office early in the morning, but his paperwork got buried under a pile of papers, and the lawyer of Mr. Bell brought his documents in after lunch, and by luck, they got filed first."[16]

16 Kuroski, John. "6 World-Changing Inventions You've Been Crediting To The Wrong Person." All That's Interesting, March 7, 2016. https://allthatsinteresting.com/famous-inventors.

So sometimes you don't have to be the first one, but maybe just in the right place at the right time. At least it is worth trying because you never know when the right time and place might happen.

How To Crack This Wall

I told my readers a similar story about this, but I love mentioning it here again.

Before I realized my passion and my true calling, I created a group for women who felt they could do better in life. I would post ideas and articles to my new group. A few of my friends commented that they were so proud to see me grow from a waitress to a life coach.

"Life coach?" Am I a life coach? I didn't know anything about what life coaching was.

Funny thing, though... I google everything, but the idea to google "What is a life coach?" didn't visit me for at least four months. I am glad because I might have quit before I started, now that I know how many life coaches are out there. I think there was a great reason for that. I had four months to cook up my idea independently with the help of several books on coaching.

Now I know there are probably a million different coaches out there, but I still have my spot under the sun and my clients as well.

So you can start by saying something like:

Everyone, including me, has their spot under the sun.

Ask yourself these questions:

What makes me think that if someone else does it, I can't?

What do I have that is unique in this field?

Why will people work with me or buy it from me?

Remember, sometimes your personal story is enough to be unique or different.

THEIR THINKING IS DIFFERENT

We all think in different ways. Our thinking is based on where we grew up, our environment, our culture, and our family. Personality plays a significant role in all of it as well.

Have you heard of personality tests? I am sure you have. Big companies love to use them before they even hire you. They often ask you to take a test as a part of your application because they want to know how you fit this position and if you have the required qualities. There are a few tests that are really popular, like DISC and Myers-Briggs.

I am sharing this with you because, based on your personality, you act, make decisions, and understand others.

For example, someone with a personality D–Dominant will say everything in a concise and straight-to-the-point way. They think that everyone should understand them, but S–Steadiness and C–Compliance will need much more information to make anything out of it.

Don't be surprised if people around you think differently and not like you. Your thinking might be exactly what they need. Share your point of view, explain what you are trying to accomplish as best as possible, and see where it takes you.

Why It Happens

I would love to share with you about a team of maintenance people I put together as Community Association Manager. It was a great team. I don't know if they still work together or went different ways. But I had to communicate with every one of them differently. Sometimes they would get frustrated that they misunderstood each other about a job assignment. They each had different skills, but when there was the right communicator between them all, they were a great team to work with, reliable and responsible.

How To Crack This Wall

You can start by saying something like:

Everyone thinks differently, but it doesn't mean they will not understand my perspective.

This could be the most frustrating wall to stop you from believing that your way will fit in or stand out. You need to learn to be a better communicator, and to understand people's personalities and the best way to talk to one person or the other. Once you find the right way to talk to the right person, you can talk to anyone and interpret your idea in their language.

Ask yourself these questions:

What am I trying to get across, and to whom?

What would be the best method to deliver my thinking in a way they would understand?

What do I need to learn to be a better communicator?

THEY DON'T TAKE RESPONSIBILITY

This wall can come in a few different shapes and forms. It might sound like this: They don't take responsibility, so I can't either, or Because they don't take responsibility for their life, it slows me down in my achievements.

I see this might be frustrating. I saw this happen with some of my clients. While they are trying to better themselves, a sister, brother, or old friend will show up in a problematic situation asking for more help than my clients can give, and all because they refuse to take responsibility for their own lives.

People like that expect someone else to come and save them: you.

It is great to help people when they are in need. It is powerful to be kind. People will remember that, and even if not, your kindness will find a way back to you one day. Compassion, love, and humanity are what this world is about and should be driven by without a doubt. But there is nothing wrong with taking care of yourself first, so you can better help others.

"If you want to have enough to give to others, you will need to take care of yourself first. A tree that refuses water and sunlight for itself can't bear fruit for others."—**Emily Maroutian**

I remember seeing people who faced this wall, confused and lost. They didn't know how to help the person and were afraid to say no or establish some boundaries that would have benefited both.

Why It Happens

It takes a mature mind to take responsibility for one's own life. Some people have it naturally, and some were not raised the right way to accept responsibility for their own lives when the time comes.

Remember one thing: you can only help a person if they ask and want to work on it themselves, like truly having a burning desire to change something about themselves and their life.

From my experience, don't waste your time if not all these components are there. You might be coming from the best place in your heart, but your efforts will be wasted and not remembered if the person is not ready.

How To Crack This Wall

Set boundaries, strong ones. Explain to everyone who is involved what you can do for them and what you cannot. Don't try to teach anyone if they are not ready for it. Remember, the only person you can change is yourself. You might influence others to change, but you can't force it on them.

You can start by saying something like:

I am responsible for my life, and the only person I can change is me.

Ask yourself these questions:

How does it influence me?

What am I trying to prove?

How can I change myself to get the result I want?

THEIR VALUES/BELIEFS
ARE DIFFERENT

This wall might be standing close to the "Their Thinking Is Different" wall.

Our values and beliefs are important. They are the way we live our lives and approach our careers. Each person's values and beliefs, consciously or not, influence their decisions and everything they do and have in life. Values and beliefs determine our priorities.

Life is usually way more satisfying when what you do and the way you behave matches your personal values and beliefs. But when these don't align, that's when things feel wrong, and it seems like everything is falling apart. It will drive you crazy, and you will feel out of place or completely lost.

Getting your point across or making people understand and support you could be difficult if you end up in an environment with absolutely different values. For example, working for a company whose values and beliefs differ from yours can be a challenge.

I see it with the younger generation. They were raised differently. I remember before it used to be, "Like it or not, just do your job." But now, especially with our world shifting so much, I see how intelligent young people value their time and freedom. They would refuse to work 40 hours a week or 8 hours a day if they knew they could complete the tasks faster. They struggle to work for a company that just wants their time, whether they are productive or not.

Why It Happens

We are all raised by different families in different environments, and our values are built on what we learn and want from life. Our values do change as our life progresses. What you value at 15 years old might not be as important at 30 or 45.

Similarly, one company's values might be based on a few people who run it. They might align for one team member and contradict with others'. Just like for those young people, a company who wants loyalty for life and values that as a priority absolutely does not support their values for freedom and curiosity to explore.

How To Crack This Wall

Respect other people's values and beliefs, but don't fixate on the people who think that theirs are the only correct ones and that you need to follow them as well. Find what is important to you. Then see what you have in common or find an environment where people have similar values.

To understand yourself deeper, recognize your personal values and beliefs. Beliefs are easier to shift, values not as much.

Here is a short list of personal values that you might find useful:

Family, Freedom, Security, Loyalty, Intelligence, Connection, Creativity, Humanity, Success, Respect, Honesty, Adventure, Kindness, Career, Contribution, Spiritualism, Professionalism, Relationships, Knowledge, Prosperity, Wellness, Gratitude, Grace, Love, Openness, Courage, Flexibility.

There are many more values. These are just a few examples for your reference.

Ask yourself these questions to understand your personal values:

What's missing from my life?

What do I spend my free time on?

What would I do if there were no limitations?

What values should someone have to align with mine?

What do I appreciate the most in people?

What quality is most important when I communicate with someone?

THEY DON'T WANT ME TO CHANGE

I have hit this wall before. It could be a struggle for the people around us when we grow personally and professionally, especially if their personal development is slower than ours or nonexistent. Some people get stuck in one spot and get so comfortable in their prison that any growth seems unnecessary and impossible. They don't see any need to do something different or something that might change their beliefs or understanding of life. They almost think they know it all and there is nothing new for them, which we already know is a delusion.

But when you start changing, even if you don't force your change on anyone else, something magical and inexplicable starts to happen. Energy is contagious. Your change will impact others around you. It doesn't matter if they want it or not. At least, you will make them feel uncomfortable in some way. It is not because of you. It is just fear of the unknown.

I am sure you heard of the famous flight-or-fight response, "an automatic physiological reaction to an event that is perceived as stressful or frightening."[17] For most of us, any change, even a positive one, is a stressful event because our brain is made to fear the unknown. We will reject or resist new things for not knowing what will happen as a result.

Why It Happens

According to Changes Psychology:

"Our brain has one part that is responsible for planning, organizing, thinking logically, reasoning, and managing emotions. It is also known as the 'higher brain,' 'rational brain,' or the 'upstairs brain.'"[18]

---

17 Psychology Tools. "Resource." Accessed July 30, 2023. https://www.psychologytools.com/resource/.
18 Team, Changes Psychology. "What Part of the Brain Controls Behavior and Emotions? - Changes Child Psychology Slug." *Changes Child Psychology* (blog), July 13, 2017. https://changespsychology.com.au/brain-emotions-behaviours/.

It also takes time to develop, to be a bit more specific, until you are 25 years old. That is why we do so many stupid and emotional things before the age of 25. Remembering myself, jumping off a cliff or getting a tattoo was not a problem. Now it would take me much longer to make the plunge.

If you are over 25 years old, you probably just thought if we have the so-called "upstairs brain," we should have the "downstairs brain." If you did, you are absolutely right. That part of the brain is responsible for emotions and memories, and overemphasizes everything to get the molecules of emotion to your entire body. This is the simplest way to explain it. This part of the brain loves to overreact… a lot, and it takes emotional intelligence to change your response from the downstairs brain to the upstairs brain. And like anything in our lives, you need to practice regularly to get better at it.

Why do I tell you all this mumbo jumbo about the brain? So you can understand that our brain is built that way, and if your change puts any stress on someone who is in your direct circle, then most likely you will get a response: resist in any possible way (fight) or run from it (flight).

And you might be stunned by what a person might do under the influence of the "downstairs brain."

How To Crack This Wall

In my life, I found only a few approaches that work:

Try to explain not in one sentence but with a lot of reasoning and facts why you need to change, and why it is important to you and for that person as well. Use as many examples as you can. Then ask them as many questions as possible on what makes them think this or that way. What and How questions are best here. Don't criticize, and be patient. No guarantees it will work, but you can try.

Keep on changing. People get used to everything, faster to good things, slower to bad, but literally to everything. So it might take some time, but they will get used to the new version of you as well.

My husband is a very stable person and doesn't like change at all. Even something simple like changing the placement of a chair or something else will throw him off-balance and make him question why it was done. But a week passes by, and he already likes it in its new place.

You can start by saying something like:

I am responsible for my personal development, and not everyone might understand me.

Ask yourself these questions:

What am I afraid of by this change?

How do people around me react?

What are they afraid of or uncomfortable with?

Why is the change important to me?

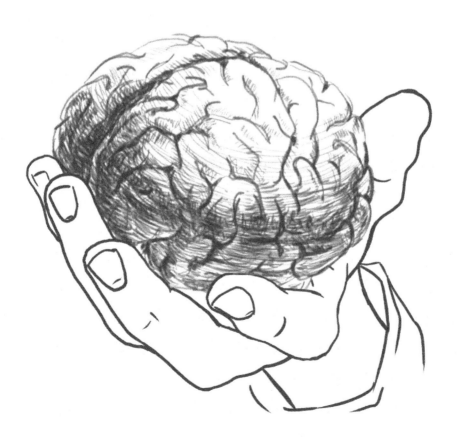

PEOPLE WANT TO TAKE ADVANTAGE OF ME

Sometimes we all feel that way. We are trying to help someone, and they start to use more of our goodwill than we meant to offer.

"You did this for me a few times, and now I feel like it is a new normal, so you need to continue to do this all the time."

Have you had this situation before?

Here's another scenario:

You have a great talent, and someone uses it to make money. And you again feel like you are being taken advantage of. So maybe at one point, you decide enough is enough. You stop producing your art and stop helping others all because of that wall. But the one person you hurt the most is yourself. You also hurt the world, who will miss your kindness and your talent.

Not every kindness will be received by someone who appreciates it and will pay it forward one day. Not every talented person can manage themselves well enough to make money.

Stories To Break The Wall

Colonel Parker is best known as Elvis Presley's manager. But this wasn't his real name; his most significant talent was managing other people's talents. I don't know if we can say that he took advantage of other people's skills. Whatever the case may be, the world might never have known Elvis Presley the way we did if it wasn't for this guy behind the scenes.

If you are from a younger generation reading this book, you probably just asked who Elvis Presley is. Known as the "King of Rock and Roll," he had an incredible impact on cultural life and was known all over the world, even years after his death. I was born after his death and still got to know his songs and story. His life will be in books, movies, and museums for generations.

How To Crack This Wall

Remember, you can't fix others, but you can do what you do best and believe it will be remembered and appreciated by the right people at the right time.

One more lesson that helps me is to give when you see a need for it without expecting anything in return. If you don't see a need, help when asked, but just enough and do not overextend yourself.

You can start by saying something like:

I get what I give, and others too.

Ask yourself these questions:

What makes me think they want to take advantage of me?

What if I stopped doing what I do?

What results would I get?

How can I turn this around in a positive way?

THEY MAKE MY LIFE COMPLICATED

You will not believe how many times I have heard this from my clients. "Everything could be so much better," they say, "but they make my life complicated," whoever "they" are. The list never ends: parents, adult kids, managers, relatives, and co-workers. People start to think they would be better off by themselves. Sometimes it might be true. But most of the time, the real problem is not caused by someone else.

As with all other walls, this one is stopping you from doing something big, meaningful, something that you are passionate about. The explanation… or, let's call things by the right name… excuse sounds reasonable enough: "I could do this and that, but they take all my time and cause all the headache."

Okay, just to be clear: sometimes we sacrifice part of our life, our time, for something greater or meaningful to us, like caring for a sick family member. It is a conscious decision and is made with kindness. It is absolutely different.

Why It Happens

We always have time for what is really important to us. The problem is that we often don't know what that is, so we waste, squander, dwindle, and decimate our time on everything else and everyone else, then blame them for taking it away from us and MAKING OUR LIFE COMPLICATED.

And, of course, we give another 100 excuses to take ourselves out of the picture and so we don't need to change anything about ourselves. We are angry, we are defensive, and so much more, but we continue with the same behavior patterns.

No one likes to admit they made a mistake, apologize for it, and then forgive themselves because it takes work, and it is much easier to push it on someone else like we usually do. Only a mentally and emotionally mature person will take full responsibility for his actions and all the results of them.

When you say, "I was late because of traffic," instead, you changed your clothes three times and left the house late.

And when you say, "They asked me to do this and that, and I didn't finish what was really important," instead, you could not find the courage to say no.

How To Crack This Wall

Sorry, I am just going to dump this one on you.

The only person who is responsible for your life and your time after you turn 18 is… drumroll… YOU.

Once we have this part clear, let's go to the next one.

I know we are talking about breaking walls in our minds, and I know it might sound weird to read this in a book, but sometimes we need to create invisible walls on the outside. I'm not referring to actual walls, but rather a set of rules to protect your time. You probably already know the word I am about to type. It is boundaries.

A boundary is an invisible line that helps you filter what is okay to get in and out. There are several types of boundaries, including physical, emotional, intellectual, material, and time.

Now, don't be afraid to use them to break the wall of "They make my life complicated."

I know it sounds crazy to say you can break internal walls by setting external walls or limits. But it works. It is almost like giving yourself more space for movement.

You can start by saying something like:

It is okay to have and set boundaries.

Ask yourself these questions:

What does responsibility mean to me?

What boundaries do I need in my life?

THEY HAVE TOO MANY OPINIONS ABOUT ME

I am sure growing up, people used to tell you who you should become. You might even have had a strong opinion that you wanted to be in this one specific profession, but your parents would say things like, "This is not a job for a woman (or a man); this is not a profession, it is a hobby; you can't make money with it; you are in the family of [insert family business], and this is your only option." Parents will have their opinions about you because they think they know better, know what is good for you, and want the best for you. Then not just your parents but your friends, your family, your spouse, etc.… they all think they know better than you. But do they?

Other people's opinions might feel harsh and pull at you from all directions, and by the time you listen to them, you are trying to remember your own opinion. Did you even have one, or did you just listen to the first person who gave theirs?

Why is this a wall? Because, like all others, it stops you from being you and discovering your purpose, passion, and understanding of what you are here for.

Why It Happens

Have you ever seen a crab trap?

Well, if not, usually it is a simple wire box with a few round openings, nothing complicated. If you tried to catch a fish with it, you probably would not be lucky enough because if it could get in, it could get out too. But it is not the same with crabs. When the box gets full of crabs, if one tries to get out by crawling through the same opening, other crabs will pull it back in. And, apparently, you don't even need a trap for that. Just a bucket is enough. The result will be the same! So it's easy to get out, but not if everyone is holding you back either by their opinions or actions.

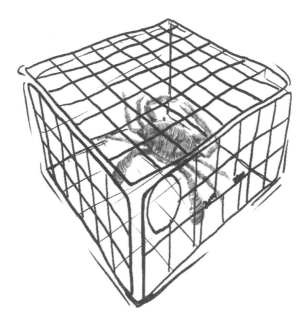

There are a lot of people who do wish you well, and they will offer their best opinion about your life from their experience. ABOUT **YOUR** LIFE FROM **THEIR** EXPERIENCE.

But a lot of other people are just like those crabs. They might intentionally keep you at the same level as theirs for many reasons, even if it means you will boil together…

How To Crack This Wall

Opinions are not always bad. I often go to my friends and people I trust to get their opinion on my new idea, new speech, etc. I will listen to what they think, and I decide whether to implement their advice or just go with my gut feeling that what I have is the right option.

Listen to others, listen… it doesn't mean follow or obey. Listen, take it in, and see if any of it is helpful to you. Do your own research, and ask yourself a lot of questions. Dig deep into what is important to you.

We are all very different, and what works for your uncle Eddie most likely will not work for you. But putting several things together might be exactly what you need.

You can start by saying something like:

I can listen to other opinions and create my own.

Ask yourself these questions:

What is my opinion right now?

What feels pushy from others?

What do I think is the best outcome for myself?

What opinions make me feel like I am in the crab trap?

THEY COMPARE ME TO OTHERS

*"I want you to know that you are good enough. That every time you give your best, it is enough. Once you stop worrying about what others think and instead focus on yourself, your life will change for the better. You deserve to be confident in who you are and not worry about what other people think."—***Kateryna Armenta**

It is in our blood. We love to compare things, people, ourselves to others, and our grass to the neighbors'. A lot of the time, comparison serves us. We can see that someone already did it and be inspired to do more, be better, and give it another chance. Why not, right?

But comparison can also be harmful. One example I remember well I am sure you are guilty of too. When I was growing up, a lot of parents used to say, "Look at this other child; he is better at sports, at school, with friends, and can do better things. He is so perfect and does everything right. Why can't you be like that?"

My friend's parents often did that, using me as an example. And let me say that I was not perfect by any means. Mainly I was just more organized, but I've always been like that. I lost a friend to comparison. She was so tired of hearing my name that she didn't even want to see me because, in the back of her mind, all she heard was her mother's words.

Now I hear a lot about our generation, especially those of us from post-Soviet Union territories, who had that experience. It grew into a giant wall of being not enough and that someone around the corner was better. From this wall, we develop our lives in two ways: either we are afraid to start anything because what is the point if someone is always better? Or on the other side, we run on the treadmill of dissatisfaction, proving to ourselves and all those voices in the back of our minds that we can be better than them or at least at the same level, even if that is not what we really want. We could be absolutely okay with less, but we keep running by trying to prove something to no one.

Why It Happens

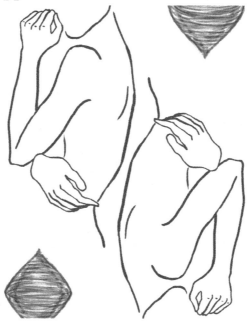

We, people, love to compare. Let's admit it is a drive for progress. But—and there is always a but—we can use it for our own development, or we can use it to harm our confidence or that of others. And our confidence, especially in the beginning, is very fragile; if cracked or damaged, it can take years of deep work to rebuild it.

How To Crack This Wall

It is difficult to change others and impossible to control what they say or do. But you can stand up for yourself and your truth. Ask them to stop using the language of comparing. Let them know there is no need to compare you to others, as you are different, and you will never be like someone else.

You can start by saying something like:

I will bloom on my own terms. I am unique. I don't have to be like others. I am enough.

Ask people who compare you with others these questions:

How can you help me to be a better version of myself without comparing me with others?

What gaps of your own are you trying to fill this way?

Ask yourself these questions:

How do I feel about it?

Is there something I want to improve?

If yes, what is it?

How am I unique?

PEOPLE THINK I HAVE TO HAVE IT TOGETHER

Review the wall "They Have Too Many Opinions About Me" if you skipped it. I cover several things in there that are related to this wall. Everyone has an opinion about how you should live your life and how it is supposed to be for you. But it is only you who lives your life, and only you know your struggles and why you act one way or another.

I had to pause for two weeks to write this chapter. It was perfect timing because I hit the wall I was writing about. I didn't realize it at first. But I felt I had demands to fulfill from all directions in my life. My closest family wanted me to have our house in order, dinner cooked, clothes cleaned, and to show care and love. The other part of the family was looking for emotional and financial support that I could not provide.

For a minute, I felt like a squirrel in a wheel, running to meet everyone's demands. After several weeks of running and making my way to this chapter, I froze when I read the chapter name I had planned months ago.

At the realization of hitting this wall once again, I froze. In that moment, I grasped that everyone around me expected me to fulfill their needs without asking how I was doing or feeling. And I was not doing well. I was in a dark place, running low on fuel but trying to show everyone that I could do what was expected of me.

Every morning I woke up and repeated to myself, *I am enough, it doesn't matter what other people think... even if I can't fulfill all their needs and demands.*

One morning I woke up with a big AHA moment. The wall I am writing about now, which hit me so hard that I had to pause writing altogether, was attached to one or maybe even a few of the "I Walls." Mine was "I am not good enough as..."

So what do I work on first? Which wall do I address?

Once one wall is destroyed, the walls next to it will also start to crumble.

Why It Happens

Here each gender has its own struggles, most of them rooted in cultural expectations for men and women. We are raised to believe that this is what we need to do and that it is okay for others to expect nothing less or more from us.

Then we take on additional responsibilities by playing several roles with certain expectations and demands. But we need to remember a few vital things. It is okay to say NO, it is okay to talk about your feelings and needs, and it is not selfish to love yourself.

How To Crack This Wall

We often don't have it together... someone might look like they do, but believe me, they are fighting their own struggles. My clients are living proof. Some come to me with what seems like a perfect life, with everything under control. But so often, it's the out-in-public mask that says that, but inside is a lot of suppressed negative feelings and insecurities.

Learn how to talk about your feelings in a healthy way, and learn how to listen as well.

Practice saying NO sometimes when you need to, and explain why you can't help them or do something for them.

You can start by saying something like:

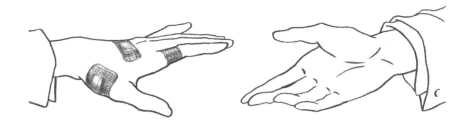

It is enough when I do my best.

Ask yourself these questions:

What makes me think that way?

What suppressed feelings or emotions do I have?

When do I need to say NO?

THEY DON'T APPRECIATE ME

Esteem is a human desire to feel accepted and valued by others. People have a need to accomplish things, then have their efforts recognized. Abraham Maslow introduced this as part of personal needs in his concept of a hierarchy of needs in 1943.

If this is the first time you are hearing about this, the needs Maslow defines in his theory are, from the bottom up: physiological, safety, love and belonging, esteem, and self-actualization.

If you are trying to fulfill your esteem need, you are looking to be appreciated and recognized. You might think of giving up when all your incredible efforts are unrecognized and underappreciated.

But wait a second. It is not time to give up. We all love praise, but for some people, it is more important than for others. That is the first thing to remember. The second is, did you clearly communicate what is important to you? Are you serving the right people to get the appreciation you are looking for?

This is a broad topic, and it all depends on who needs to appreciate you a little bit more, according to you. Is it your family, boss, co-workers, friends, and so on?

Now based on your answer, you will make some changes not in them but in yourself, because remember, the only thing you can control and change is YOU.

Why It Happens

We seek appreciation because it fulfills our basic needs for validation, recognition, and self-worth. When we receive appreciation, it boosts our confidence and motivates us to continue performing well. Additionally, appreciation from others can also reinforce our social connections and foster a sense of belonging. However, seeking too much validation from others can become a problem if it leads to a dependence on external validation for self-worth.

That's why it's important to also cultivate a sense of self-worth and validation from within. Without it, we run into the familiar wall of "I am not enough."

How To Crack This Wall

You can start by saying something like:

I am enough as long as I give my best.

The right people will see my efforts.

Start by communicating your needs to the right people. Often, we look for other people to fulfill our needs if we cannot meet them within our closest circle. So if you are looking for appreciation on Facebook from people you only saw in a photo once or twice… check with those who live next to you.

Ask yourself these questions:

How do I want them to show appreciation?

What do I need to be appreciated for?

How can I communicate to them what is important to me?

THEY DON'T TRUST ME

The limiting belief that others don't trust you can hold you back from building strong relationships and achieving your goals.

We should believe that every human being is trustworthy until and unless he or she proves otherwise. But not everyone feels secure enough to do that. Instead, they believe trust is earned over time through consistent actions and communication. This way of trusting could stop us from reaching our goals in many areas of life and creating meaningful relationships with people we need for support and growth.

Step back to view the situation and ask yourself a lot of questions. We will get to them in a little bit.

Why It Happens

There could be different reasons why someone does not trust you. But here are a few reasons why you are facing this wall.

They might have had a bad experience in the past and were hurt or betrayed. They learned that it is not safe to trust others.

Some people may have negative beliefs about people in general, such as believing that people are inherently selfish or untrustworthy.

Some people might want to be in control. They may be afraid that others will take advantage of them if they are not in control. So they take precautions by not trusting anyone from the very beginning.

Some people may have low self-esteem and believe they are not worthy of being trusted. This can make it difficult for them to trust others because they may believe that others will not want to trust them either.

People who have experienced trauma, such as abuse or neglect, may have difficulty trusting others. But this is an intense topic.

And last but not least, you might have built this wall with some of your actions or words.

How To Crack This Wall

Rather than focusing on the belief that others don't trust you, try to identify what actions you can take to build trust and strengthen your relationships.

Remember to look into what you can control of your personal behavior to earn trust and give room to others as they might be fighting their past where they lost trust in people.

You can start by saying something like:

I can only do what is right and hope people will see it.

Ask yourself these questions:

What actions will make others trust me?

What makes me think others don't trust me?

How can I build trust one step at a time?

What do I need to work on in my personal behavior and actions?

How will I act if I know the distrust is not mine?

OTHER PEOPLE'S SKILLS AFFECT MY PERFORMANCE

My client told me she is working on a project with a group of people, and she is about to give up because she feels she puts in the most effort, and others barely do their part, if at all. It wasn't the first time I heard this from my clients and many other people.

This is a common wall. While it is true that we and our outcomes may be influenced by the skills and performance of those around us, we have the power to control our own actions and work towards our own goals regardless of the abilities of others.

Why do we look at this as a wall?

Many people gave up on their goals, work, or mission because they worked in a group or with someone who was supposed to complete one of the steps, and they felt it was unfair that they were more involved in it than anyone else.

Why It Happens

Do you feel underappreciated?

We may become less motivated to continue working on something when we feel unappreciated for our hard work.

Do you feel like no one is listening?

When our concerns are not heard or taken seriously, we may become frustrated and less likely to want to continue our work.

Do you feel like you don't have the resources to succeed?

When we feel like we do not have the resources to complete a project, we may become discouraged and less likely to want to continue working on it.

Do you feel like it is not worth your time or effort?

When we do not perceive a higher purpose in our work, we may decide to give up on it altogether.

How To Crack This Wall

It is important to remember that everyone has different motivations and reasons for doing things. Still, your skills and effort are the main factors determining your performance and your future success.

When this happens at work, the best solution is to better communicate with your manager and coworkers.

If you are working on a personal goal and hit this wall, remember why you started.

You can start by saying something like:

I can control only my own actions and skills.

Ask yourself these questions:

What is the main reason I feel that way?

How could I resolve this?

What can I do to get the outcome I need?

PART III:
Walls Of Emotions
And Feelings

*"Thoughts are the shadows of our feelings—always darker, emptier, and simpler."—**Friedrich Nietzsche***

I was excited and a little bit nervous about writing this part. This is a big dive into the ocean of the unknown that we start to uncover lake by lake.

I have to warn you that I am not a scientist and don't have a PhD in Psychology. Everything I will be writing about was learned from many books and articles, but most were obtained from observation and intuitive knowledge that came to me. I honestly have no idea how to explain it.

Many times I would tell my friends about some theory that I came up with by looking at people and situations, and they would say, "There's a name for that theory. I read about it in a book." Then they often would say, "Well, no need for you to read it; you already know it."

You will find this part of the book is different from the other three. We will not address how to crack each wall separately, but I will give a conclusion at the end of this part. This part of the book doesn't dispense medical advice or treatment for a physical, emotional, or medical problem.

But first, a word to distinguish emotions and feelings, since often we use the words interchangeably.

Emotions are short-lived experiences that change people's thoughts, actions, and physiological responses. Emotions are not conscious but instead manifest in the unconscious mind. It is like a chemical reaction that happens first. The feeling is usually a result of an emotion or a few emotions.

Feelings are both emotional experiences and physical sensations, such as hunger or pain. Feelings are a conscious experience.[19]

We can control feelings, but we can't control emotions.

Okay, let's begin this emotional journey to uncover the truth.

From about 10 years old, I started to see in the actions and words of others some hidden patterns from pain and negative feelings they experienced in their life long ago. I saw what was happening, especially with people around me, but my emotional intelligence wasn't ready to understand or explore it further.

In the last few years, when I opened a new door in my career and let my intuitive knowledge surface, I could not believe everything I had discovered. What I am about to tell you is just the tip of the iceberg, and if you want to understand these concepts better, you need to explore them in depth.

We live in a very physical world. Everything is measured by what we see with our eyes or what we can touch with our hands. But there is so much more that plays a big part in creating our world that we can't touch or see but only experience through feeling if we are conscious and aware enough.

We have lived in the physical world for so long, accepting it as absolute truth for generations, that we have forgotten our connection to so much more. Our parents and grandparents were taught to suppress or ignore their feelings, or "walk them off." I wasn't any different, and now I am peeling my own onion to get rid of some programming and avoid other consequences that usually come with it. It is an awakening, and it takes some hard work.

---

19 Fredrickson, Barbara L., and Christine Branigan. "Positive Emotions Broaden the Scope of Attention and Thought-Action Repertoires." *Cognition & Emotion*, vol. 19, no. 3, May 2005, pp. 313–32. *PubMed Central*, https://doi.org/10.1080/02699930441000238.

I intuitively knew that our buried, unprocessed, ignored, suppressed negative emotions and feelings don't die as we thought. In fact, they live on, influencing all aspects of our life, including our bodies. But now I am on a quest to find proof. I am not the first and definitely not the last, but I am glad I could support my theory with many books written by scientists and doctors in various fields.

What if I told you that our feelings and emotions have much more power and live longer than we thought? Our emotions register on many levels, including chemical and energetic.

From an energy perspective: everything around us is energy, including our thoughts, feelings, and emotions. A lot of scientists have talked about this, including Einstein. He said, "Everything is energy, and that's all there is to it. Match the frequency of the reality you want, and you cannot help but get that reality." And as we know from thermodynamics, energy cannot be created or destroyed; it can only change states. We also know that matter and energy are two sides of the same coin.

Candace B. Pert writes on the chemical perspective in her book Molecules of Emotions: "On a more global scale, these minute physiological phenomena at a cellular level can translate to large changes in behavior, physical activity, even mood."[20]

In the following chapters, we will look into certain emotions and feelings that, if buried, blocked, suppressed, or repressed, can become giant walls in your heart, mind, and your entire body.

---

20 Pert, Candace B. *Molecules of Emotion: Why You Feel the Way You Feel.* New York: Scribner, 2003.

GRIEF

Losing a friend or family member is one of the most difficult situations in life, and sometimes we just need to allow time to go through it and have a supportive shoulder to lean on.

According to Wikipedia, grief is:

"[…] the response to loss, particularly to the loss of someone or some living thing that has died, to which a bond or affection was formed. Although conventionally focused on the emotional response to loss, grief also has physical, cognitive, behavioral, social, cultural, spiritual, and philosophical dimensions."[21]

Like many other negative emotions or feelings, it doesn't come alone. It may be accompanied by pain, anguish, regret, confusion, and anger.

We used to believe grief only came from losing a person, but it also comes from losing something: a marriage, financial stability, a part of the body, a relationship, as well as status or authority.

Now, we have all heard of the five stages of grief. Kübler-Ross originally developed stages to describe the process patients with terminal illnesses go through as they come to terms with their own deaths. But then the stages were applied to everyone experiencing the loss of a loved one. Let's remember what those are.

Denial. Your first reaction is to hope it was a mistake, and you might cling to the false reality of something or someone still being there. You might isolate yourself to avoid the reality or presence of others. This stage is usually a temporary defense.

Anger. "Why me? It's not fair!"; "How can this happen to me?"; "Who is to blame?"; "Why would this happen?" After denial, you become frustrated with the situation or the person you lost.

---

21 "Grief." In *Wikipedia*, July 4, 2023. https://en.wikipedia.org/w/index.php?title=Grief&oldid=1163451399.

Bargaining. You might think you're willing to do anything and sacrifice everything if your life is restored to how it was before the loss.

Depression. "I'm so sad, why bother with anything?"; "I miss my loved one; why go on?"

Acceptance. "It's going to be okay." In the final stage, you begin to understand how you can live with it and let it go in some way.

I know grief is a strong feeling, and sometimes putting it in a nice, neat box with five stages might seem unfair. This difficult emotion can last anywhere from months to years.

But the most important thing is not to get stuck in it. The television series *Black Mirror* has one episode when a wife, out of grief, buys a computer clone of her husband. With time, she does move on but doesn't know what to do with it, so she keeps the clone in her attic as a reminder of life.

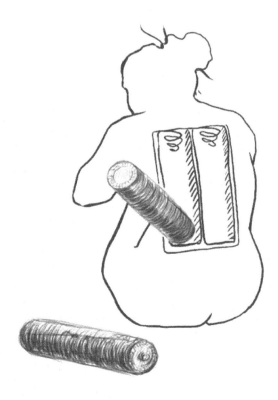

What It Does

Grief increases inflammation, which can worsen health problems you already have and cause new ones. It batters the immune system, leaving you depleted and vulnerable to infection. The heartbreak of grief can increase blood pressure and the risk of blood clots. Intense grief can alter the heart muscle so much that it causes "broken heart syndrome," a form of heart disease with the same symptoms as a heart attack.

I am sure once in your life you have heard that someone lost a loved one and shortly after died out of nowhere. When we decide there is no reason to live and hold on to grief so tightly, sending our body and the Universe or God those signals, we get what we are asking for and, it could result in "broken heart syndrome."

Remember to look at the end of this part to find a few different ways to break the walls of our negative and trapped emotions around grief and more.

GUILT

*"Nothing is more wretched than the mind of a man conscious of guilt."—**Plautus***

When you look up guilt, you will find several meanings, but most of them say that it is from shame or a feeling of doing wrong or causing harm to yourself or others, especially consciously. I will disagree a bit, and here is why.

Psychology Today says:

"People may feel guilt for various reasons, including acts they have committed (or think that they committed), a failure to do something they should have done, or thoughts that they think are morally wrong."[22]

People feel guilt much more often than described in any article or magazine. Mothers, for instance, often feel guilt for things that happened out of their control and that could not have been prevented. We feel guilty about giving some time and attention to ourselves, thinking that others need it more than us. We feel that way simply going to the gym, thinking we must cook dinner.

Guilt is a complex emotion that can be both positive and negative. It can motivate us to make amends for our mistakes, but it can also hold us back and influence our entire life, from actions we take or don't take to the way we act and what thoughts we think. Walls "I am a mess" and "I am not good enough" come from this emotion.

Guilt can be debilitating. It can make us feel ashamed, worthless, and like we are not good enough. It can also lead to anxiety, depression, loss of interest, fatigue, difficulty concentrating, social withdrawal, and other mental health problems.

---

22 "Guilt | Psychology Today." Accessed July 30, 2023. https://www.psychologytoday.com/us/basics/guilt.

Over time, people trapped in walls of guilt may develop a sense of inadequacy. They may feel they don't deserve to move on and may engage in behaviors designed to punish themselves for their mistakes, sometimes to the point of hurting themselves physically.

I am telling you all that not to scare you but for you to understand if you have a wall of guilt that needs to be brought down as soon as possible so you can see the light at the end of the tunnel.

What It Does

In the article "The Weight of a Guilty Conscience: Subjective Body Weight as an Embodiment of Guilt," Martin V. Day and D. Ramona Bobocel explain their research about how feeling guilty equally weighs down our entire body:

"In a series of studies we asked students and members of the public to recall a time that they did something unethical. People recalled a variety of wrongdoings, such as lying, stealing or cheating. Afterward, in a separate task, we asked them to rate their subjective feeling of their own body weight as compared to their average. That is, did they feel less weight than usual, about the same weight, or more weight? We compared these responses to participants in control conditions who recalled an ethical memory, a memory of someone else's unethical actions or who were not asked to recall a memory."[23]

It not only weighs you down but may also create illnesses in different body parts, often in the liver and bladder.

---

23 Day, Martin V., and D. Ramona Bobocel. "The Weight of a Guilty Conscience: Subjective Body Weight as an Embodiment of Guilt." *PLOS ONE* 8, no. 7 (July 31, 2013): e69546. https://doi.org/10.1371/journal.pone.0069546.

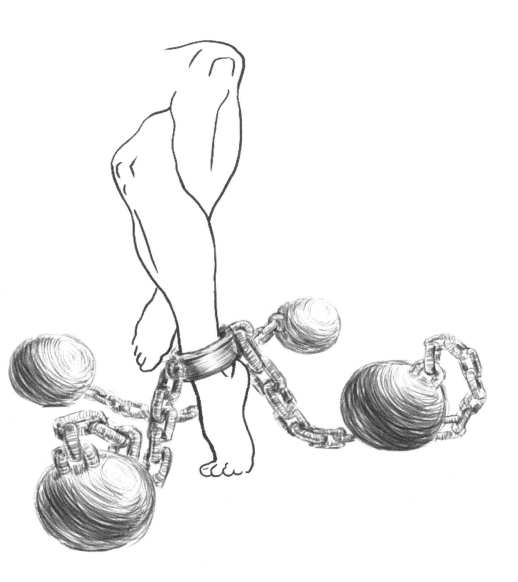

SHAME

Guilt and shame often occur together to some extent. Guilt can trigger a sense of shame in many people. If they go against their values and standards, and they recognize it, shame comes together with the guilt of doing wrong.

In 2010, a team of psychologists led by Ulrich Orth of the University of Bern studied shame in more than 2,600 volunteers between the ages of 13 and 89, most of whom lived in the US. They found not only that men and women feel shame for different reasons but also that age seems to affect how readily people experience it.[24]

Women and teenagers are more likely to feel shame than men. It might be connected with higher confidence levels in men, engraved in their DNA. As an effect, women and teenagers under the influence of shame often have low self-esteem.

"Shame—the feeling that 'I am bad' rather than simply 'I did something bad'—is one of the most primitive, universal pieces of our moral system," says June Tangney, a clinical psychology professor at George Mason University.[25]

Above is a straightforward explanation of why shame can have such a horrible impact on how we see ourselves as an individual. A wall of guilt makes us feel awful because we did something wrong. A wall of shame makes us feel like a bad person, maybe even unworthy in some way.

What It Does

Like many other negative and stressful emotions, shame triggers the sympathetic nervous system, generating the flight-fight-freeze response.

---

24 Kämmerer, Annette. "The Scientific Underpinnings and Impacts of Shame." Scientific American. Accessed July 30, 2023. https://www.scientificamerican.com/article/the-scientific-underpinnings-and-impacts-of-shame/.
25 Bourg, Jim. "June Tangney on 'Shame.'" Psychology. Accessed July 30, 2023. https://psychology.gmu.edu/articles/12362.

As a result, we might try to hide by making our bodies smaller or to fight in some way, often projecting negative emotions onto others around us.

As with any other negative emotion, if not lived through and let go, it will settle in your body and affect your behavior and perspective on life. In particular, shame experienced for a long time might manifest in illnesses that affect the sexual organs.

If this is the only wall of feelings and emotions you are reading, please don't forget to read the last chapter in this part, where I will share the secrets to breaking walls of negative feelings and emotions.

FRUSTRATION

This is the most common feeling we face and recognize in ourselves and people around us. We hear this word used a lot as well: "I felt frustrated at work today"; "My doctor canceled the appointment again... it is so frustrating." Sometimes this feeling is short-lived, and other times it is long-term.

We all face daily situations that frustrate us: standing too long in that line to buy a few groceries and someone in front of you counting 100 pennies to pay for their things, a coworker who didn't complete his part of the work and causing you to have to delay yours, the client who didn't show up for an appointment without notifying you, the neighbors' dog who barked all night, the furniture that wasn't delivered on time... there are numerous situations that make us feel frustrated.

You could also feel frustrated with yourself because you forgot the key or lost your wallet. So based on this, let's say frustration could be external or internal: external, when something from outside triggers the feeling; internal, when something on the inside or something you are responsible for triggers the same.

Most of us know how it feels, and we definitely know when to use the word to describe it. But what does it really mean? Frustration is "the unpleasant experience when things are not working the way you want them to work."[26] It can come together with anger. Your frustration can build into a rage.

We understand short-term frustration well, but how does long-term frustration show up? Maybe missing out on friendship frustrates you for years, or your imperfect relationship, and there could be so much more.

---

26 Wierzbicka, Anna. *Emotions across Languages and Cultures: Diversity and Universals.* Studies in Emotion and Social Interaction. Cambridge [England] ; New York : Paris: Cambridge University Press ; Editions de la Maison des sciences de l'homme, 1999.

There are a few things I want to share here if you get frustrated, whether short-term or long-term, internal or external. Several trapped emotions feed this feeling.

What It Does

I wish more studies were done on how our emotions influence our bodies. So far, all we know for sure is that stress in any of its forms, including all the emotions and feelings I have listed in this book and more, can grow into illness. I will talk more in the last chapter about this topic.

For now, psychologists agree that negative feelings and emotions influence our mental health in many ways. Frustration in particular can bring on anger, aggression, a feeling of giving up, loss of confidence, depression, and other issues like stress eating, alcohol abuse, and other addictive behaviors.

ANGER

*"Anybody can become angry—that is easy, but to be angry with the right person and to the right degree and at the right time and for the right purpose, and in the right way—that is not within everybody's power and is not easy."—**Aristotle***

When you feel angry, your body goes through a number of physical changes. Your heart rate and blood pressure increase, your muscles tense up, and your breathing becomes faster. Actually, that happens when you experience several other negative emotions, all thanks to the brain's natural response to danger. You get the rush of emotion through your body, and your brain screams, "Danger... danger, we must do something immediately!"

People express anger in a few different ways. Some may become violent, while others become passive-aggressive. Anger is often masking a deeper emotion that has been bothering you for years and now leaks out as this stinky anger.

I will share with you something very private here. At one point, my husband had to take an anger management class. His response was to fight, and there was no logical brain involved. It was almost as if a switch would go off, and he could not understand what he was doing until it was done. I have never experienced violence from him directly, but he broke doors and other stuff as well. Now he has learned to take time and breathe slowly to activate his logical brain and not to act on the fight-or-flight response.

When writing this part, I remembered the TV show Working Moms. In one season, a psychotherapist was dealing with her own anger and had to do an anger management class herself. First, the most crucial step was admitting why she was angry and why it had been piling up inside her all this time. By becoming aware of our triggers and learning to recognize the early signs of anger, we can manage our emotions before they escalate.

What It Does

Building a higher and thicker wall of anger can lower immune function and increase the risk of developing a chronic illness. Anger tends to impact the heart and head. In one report, researchers found that:

"[…]healthy people who are often angry or hostile are 19% more likely to get heart disease than calmer people. Among people with heart disease, those who usually feel angry or hostile fared worse than others."[27]

Anger can increase your risk of heart attack, high blood pressure, stroke, liver illnesses, and headaches, and contributes to a stressful life overall with tense relationships.

---

27 Kam, Katherine. "How Anger Can Hurt Your Heart." WebMD. Accessed July 30, 2023. https://www.webmd.com/balance/stress-management/features/how-anger-hurts-your-heart.

JEALOUSY/ENVY

Even though these are negative emotions that may hold us prisoner, if interpreted right and lived through, they can have a positive impact. Let's see what psychologists say about it.

In "The Evolutionary Psychology of Envy and Jealousy" from the magazine *Frontiers of Psychology*, Vilayanur S. Ramachandran and Baland Jalal write:

"You are often consciously aware of being jealous or envious of someone, but sometimes the actual reasons for the envy are buried in your unconscious and disguised by rationalizations. Envy and jealousy kick in as a gut reaction in your emotional/evaluative system long before you become conscious of it.

"What is the evolutionary logic that drives envy; e.g., the fact that you envy your neighbor more than Bill Gates? The answer is that the whole purpose of envy is to motivate you into action either by independently trying harder (envy) or by coveting and stealing what the other has (jealousy). This is why jealousy has an aggressive component, but envy is more positive sometimes even being tinged with admiration."[28]

We can experience these emotions in so many aspects of our life, including relationships, belonging, and status. I used to hurt myself by being jealous, and it seemed like it was eating me from the inside until I realized why it was there and why God or the Universe gifted us this powerful emotion. It was created to reinforce progress in our life.

At its core, jealousy is often driven by a fear of losing something or someone that is perceived as valuable or by not having something that others do. If you are getting that jealous feeling in your gut, you have a desire to get something for yourself. Now consider the questions: How can you

---

28 Ramachandran, Vilayanur S., and Baland Jalal. "The Evolutionary Psychology of Envy and Jealousy." *Frontiers in Psychology* 8 (2017). https://www.frontiersin.org/articles/10.3389/fpsyg.2017.01619.

make it possible? What are you jealous of, really? If you attain what you desire, will you feel happier and fulfilled? Can you learn from the person or situation how to achieve the same results? Or can you let it go?

What It Does

A study found that women in the throes of jealousy had trouble spotting obvious objects. The greater their jealousy, the harder it was for them to see these objects. Researchers believe that jealousy, envy, and anger have similar effects on our awareness if bottled up for extended periods.

Emotion is a complicated topic, and not many researchers go deep enough to explore all the ins and outs of it. But looking at everything from an energy perspective makes more sense.

DISAPPOINTMENT

"Disappointment is a sort of bankruptcy—the bankruptcy of a soul that expends too much in hope and expectation."—**Eric Hoffer**

Everyone experiences disappointment at some point in their lives. Sadness or dissatisfaction arises when things do not go as expected or desired. Personal failures, unmet expectations, broken promises, and lost opportunities can all cause disappointment.

But disappointment it is not a sign of weakness. Like any other negative emotion, it exists for a reason; if recognized and understood, disappointment can motivate us and bring about positive changes.

We experience disappointment in three ways:

I am disappointing: I do not live up to other people's expectations.

I am disappointed: Other people do not live up to my expectations of them.

I disappoint: I can tolerate disappointment. I am okay with disappointing others in certain situations.

Usually, the second and third ways are easier to process and let go of unless in very personal cases, like being disappointed in a relationship in which you invested heavily. Of course, disappointment can help build all the other walls of negative emotions.

But the first one often catches us on a much deeper level and can also impact our mental health.

What It Does

"It's an evolutionary response to maximize our survival—we feel disappointment deeply so we don't make the same mistake again in the future," says neuroscientist Christophe Proulx.[29]

Usually, disappointment, like any other emotion, is processed and let go of. But if we get stuck in it, we start by withdrawing, avoiding our feelings, attacking ourselves, and as a result, attacking others around us.

---

29 Dold, Kristen. "What Disappointing News Does to Your Body." *Vice* (blog), December 20, 2016. https://www.vice.com/en/article/bmn3w4/what-disappointing-news-does-to-your-body.

ENTITLEMENT

Entitlement is more a feeling than an emotion, and it wasn't researched as deeply as other emotions and feelings I have discussed.

Entitlement is a belief that one is inherently deserving of privileges or special treatment. Entitlement is generally selfish. It demands much, and it gives little or nothing.

I wanted to bring this up because while living in the US for 10 years, I have seen this feeling a lot in younger generations. Kids anywhere from 7 to 18 seem to think they are entitled to everything they want. A lot of parents overdeliver, causing an aftermath of disappointment from the ingratitude of their children. So many negative walls are being built…

"When we replace a sense of service and gratitude with a sense of entitlement and expectation, we quickly see the demise of our relationships, society, and economy."—***Steve Maraboli,*** **Unapologetically You: Reflections on Life and the Human Experience**

How can you use entitlement for good?

You are part of an intelligent Universe. If you believe that, then an intelligent entity created you with a purpose in mind. You are entitled to live this life with purpose, and no one can take it from you. You can use this feeling in a positive way by being grateful for what you have and what you experience but not entitled to anything.

I often see teenagers, after leaving their homes where their parents supported their feeling of entitlement, have difficulty beginning life on their own with the realization that not every wish is granted without some work being done.

You might remember that the Bible says to ask, and it will be given to you. But often we only see what we want to see. The Bible says a lot too about doing the work that needs to be done, like: you shall eat the fruit of the labor of your hands.

Teach your children to work and be grateful for what they receive and for what you provide for them.

What It Does

Believing that you are entitled to more than others and that you deserve to be treated better than anyone else can eventually result in long-term damage to your relationships, unhappiness, jealousy, disappointment, and depression.

According to *WebMD*:

"Feeling entitled to something and the disappointment that follows when you don't get what you want can reinforce entitled behavior. This typically follows a vicious three-step cycle:

When you're entitled, you're always vulnerable to the threat of unmet expectations.

When your expectations aren't met, it can lead to dissatisfaction and other emotions like anger and a sense of being cheated.

When you're distressed, you try to fix the situation and console yourself. This results in self-reassurance that you deserve everything you've ever wanted, which reinforces the same entitled behavior."[30]

---

30 Contributors, WebMD Editorial. "What Is an Entitlement Mentality?" WebMD. Accessed July 30, 2023. https://www.webmd.com/mental-health/what-is-an-entitlement-mentality.

LONELINESS

I was excited to get to this wall and bring you the good news. I know this might sound religious, "the good news." But it is not that religious. In fact, it is natural if you really look deep into it.

I had to look into statistics, and they are shocking. I want to give you some numbers here so you can understand why we need to look into what is happening and to heal this negative energy in our minds and body.

According to statistics compiled by *Social Self*, when asked how often they felt lonely, 50% of Generation X (born 1961–1981) respondents reported sometimes or always feeling lonely (US, YouGov, 2019). Among Millennials (born 1982–1999), 65% sometimes or always feel lonely (US, YouGov, 2019). Generation Z (born 1997–2012) is the loneliest age group (US, Cigna, 2018).[31]

---

31 SocialSelf. "Loneliness Statistics 2022: Demographics, USA & Worldwide." Accessed July 31, 2023. https://socialself.com/loneliness-statistics/.

I am just guessing, but social media use could be connected to these statistics: 34% of children aged 12–17 admit to being cyberbullied. 73% of very heavy social media users feel lonely compared to 52% of light users who feel lonely.

Overall, 36% of Americans—including 61% of young adults and 51% of mothers with young children—feel serious loneliness.[32]

Now think about this: it is not because they are alone. About 30%–40% of married people feel lonely too.

Are we in an epidemic of loneliness? Could it be linked to developing technologies and the increased use of virtual life experiences?

Did you know that babies who are not held and hugged enough can stop growing and even die if it continues for too long? If loneliness affects babies, does it affect adults this way too?

I know I promised good news at the beginning. The good news is that we are never alone. And I am not even talking about your friends and family or people in general. We need society to support us, but if we find that our souls and spirits are connected to everything around us, we will never feel lonely again. I know we need to go through a spiritual journey to realize that, and it is not a religious matter.

What It Does

"What's so powerful about loneliness is it affects everything—every aspect of health and well-being," says Angelina Sutin, PhD, a professor of psychology at Florida State University in Tallahassee.[33]

As with many other negative emotions over a long span of time, loneliness may increase your chances for depreciation, poor sleep, unhealthy habits like substance abuse, heart attack, inflammation, and even dementia.

---

32 Pandey, Erica. "Lonely America." Axios Finish Line, n.d. https://www.axios.com/2022/10/26/loneliness-pandemic-america-phone-calls.
33 EverydayHealth.com. "The Health Risks of Loneliness: What the Science Says," February 25, 2022. https://www.everydayhealth.com/wellness/united-states-of-stress/what-toll-does-loneliness-take-on-our-health/.

RESENTMENT

What is resentment? The simplest definition is a feeling of being mistreated. A person experiencing resentment often feels other negative emotions, including anger, disappointment, bitterness, and sadness.

With resentment, we tend to hold on to our past, reliving what happened and what makes us feel that way triggers more of all the negative walls to rise even higher.

One of the challenges of dealing with resentment is that it can be difficult to let go of. We may feel justified in our anger and believe that holding onto it protects us from further harm. However, in reality, holding onto resentment can harm our well-being.

You may feel resentful for a moment or for a long period of time in your life. Especially as we grow wiser and have more years on this Earth, looking back and seeing that we have been treated unfairly for a part of our life can bring up resentment along with remorse and regret. Wishing that we had acted differently earlier, we often add self-blame to the other walls we have built.

What It Does

According to the University of New Hampshire:

"By refusing to give up a "justified resentment," you may believe that you are punishing the person who wronged you. However, resentful behavior actually leads you to feel hurt and victimized again, disempowered. To let go of resentment would be to experience increased freedom and mental health."[34]

Resentment also has physical effects, such as increasing your heart rate, blood pressure, and muscle tension. Over time, these physical responses can lead to chronic health problems.

There is one way out of resentment: stop punishing yourself and forgive everyone involved. You might wonder why you should forgive this person for everything that happened to you or to someone you love. Forgiveness has more power than you think, according to Johns Hopkins:

"Numerous studies have found that the act of forgiveness can reap huge rewards for your health, lowering the risk of heart attack; improving cholesterol levels and sleep; and reducing pain, blood pressure, and levels of anxiety, depression, and stress. And research points to an increase in the forgiveness-health connection as you age."[35]

*"As smoking is to the lungs, so is resentment to the soul; even one puff is bad for you." —**Elizabeth Gilbert***

---

34 Psychological & Counseling Services. "Resentment and Forgiveness," March 10, 2020. https://www.unh.edu/pacs/resentment-forgiveness.
35 "Forgiveness: Your Health Depends on It," November 1, 2021. https://www.hopkinsmedicine.org/health/wellness-and-prevention/forgiveness-your-health-depends-on-it.

BITTERNESS

"Bitterness is venom that consumes its host."—**Matshona Dhliwayo**

You may say that resentment and bitterness are the same thing. They often come as a pair, but I disagree with calling those two the same. When resentment is directed at a specific person or situation, you are holding on to a specific thing or believing that someone did you wrong.

Bitterness does not always come from a specific situation. Bitterness might be built on the imagined hurt or a feeling that you were treated wrong somehow, but often you can't explain how. You might feel bitter because you are not successful the way you expected, or sometimes even because you don't have something you want but feel like you deserve it. Bitterness can be the outcome of resentment when you think that you have forgiven, but the resentment is still rooted in your heart.

People with bitterness in their hearts and thoughts are sad and lack a lust for life.

What It Does

Bitterness is the bad apple that spoils the bunch. If not removed, it will eventually rot the entire basket of good fruit. That basket is you and your heart.

I can't explain why, but I feel like this hurt is often responsible for creating cancer cells in our bodies. If getting rid of bitterness can cure cancer, why not try? Because it is just like that rotten apple placed inside that eats us alive or tries to rot everything around it. This is just some insight I got while writing.

HELPLESSNESS

Have you experienced this before, like nothing you did helped or resolved the problem, or gave you an exit from an unwanted situation? I did, and I felt like I could do nothing to get out. This is how helplessness feels. It seems like you lost control and can't gain it back.

Before we talk more about this emotion, I will share with you how the feeling of control influences our life. In psychology, they use the term locus of control. There is internal and external locus of control.

People with an internal locus take responsibility and feel like they control their destiny. As you guessed, external is quite the opposite—passing control to everything and everyone around them. In this book, the concept of locus of control is represented too in the "I Walls" and "They Walls." Many studies show that people with an internal locus of control are happier and more successful in life.

Now imagine that you feel like any control was taken away from you, and you set your bricks one by one on the tall wall of helplessness, not knowing how to take back control.

Helplessness is feeling stuck, but sometimes we are stuck in feeling helpless. Psychologists call it learned helplessness:

"The term was first used in 1967 by the American psychologists Martin Seligman and Steven Maier. The pair were conducting research on animal behavior that involved delivering electric shocks to dogs. Dogs who learned that they couldn't escape the shock stopped trying in subsequent experiments, even when it became possible to avoid the shock by jumping over a barrier."[36]

You might say how a dog's behavior is connected to people's behavior. More studies have been done, and apparently, people do the same thing. If we get into a situation where we can't do anything for some time,

---

36 "Learned Helplessness | Psychology Today." Accessed July 31, 2023. https://www.psychologytoday.com/us/basics/learned-helplessness.

eventually, we stop trying. And with that comes low self-esteem, frustration, passivity, lack of effort, and giving up on anything we start.

What It Does

Suppose helplessness is not addressed and becomes a chronic state of mind. In that case, it can lead to adult-entitled dependence (AED) and mental health disorders like anxiety, depression, and post-traumatic stress disorder. As any other negative emotions contributing to our stress levels, helplessness can manifest in diseases related to the stomach and heart.

It can be difficult and distressing to experience, but overcoming helplessness and regaining control over your life is possible.

DOUBT/CONFUSION

"Our doubts are traitors, and make us lose the good we oft might win, by fearing to attempt."—**William Shakespeare,** Measure for Measure

A few weeks ago, one of my clients wasn't feeling well and had to reschedule our session several times. When I opened the Zoom call at the set time and waited for 15 minutes in vain, I was confused because I knew it was the right time, but I doubted myself, thinking I missed some part of the communication.

Confusion and doubt are different feelings, but nevertheless, they often go together. Let me explain. As P. J. Silvia wrote in his article "Confusion and Interest: The Role of Knowledge Emotions in Aesthetic Experience," you feel confused when you receive information that you cannot match with what you already know or believe to be true.[37] Doubt, on the other hand, is the feeling of uncertainty about something. It could be something you believe or know. As you see, those feelings often come as a pair.

Those feelings are not always bad for us. Like any other negative emotion or feeling, confusion and doubt are there for a reason, and if we analyze and respond appropriately, they can bring significant positive results. Many inventions and hunts for truth began from uncertainty and doubt.

But it becomes harmful when we start to doubt our abilities to do something or try something new, or even worse, when we get confused about who we are and what we bring to this world. Self-doubt creeps in... We feel this sometimes, and often it is a sign to look deeper once again and rediscover ourselves or maybe push doubtful thoughts aside and ask, What

---

37 Silvia, Paul J. "Confusion and Interest: The Role of Knowledge Emotions in Aesthetic Experience." *Psychology of Aesthetics, Creativity, and the Arts* 4, no. 2 (May 2010): 75–80. https://doi.org/10.1037/a0017081.

if I try? What if I could do this? What if I can learn something new to make it clear again?

Self-doubt and confusion jeopardize our sense of being in control of our life, which we talked about in the previous chapter. They shake the bases of what we know and what we build our entire life upon. At times these feelings can throw off our perception of how it is supposed to be and why.

What They Do

Being stuck in self-doubt and confusion can lead to problems with anxiety and depression, weight gain, high blood pressure, chronic fatigue, and more.

Have you felt tired all the time lately? It could very well be related to the fact that you doubt yourself every step of the way. Maybe you didn't do something you felt you meant to do because your parents told you several times that you have no talent for it or that there is no money in doing what you wished to do for so long, and for whatever reason, you believed them. Maybe now, looking at someone else successfully doing that, you are confused about how they managed and why you couldn't take that first step and stop doubting yourself. As I said in my previous book: it is better to try and know that you gave it a chance than not to try and always wonder what would have happened if you did.

INSECURITY

I had to put this wall in here right after doubt and confusion. These two walls often create a corner that we run into head-on, and we stare at the two walls coming together, unable to see a way out.

What do we mean by insecurity? We discussed the feeling of not being good enough and, of course, all the thoughts that come together with this emotional wall in the first part of this book. Insecurity doesn't come alone, either. Unfortunately, most negative emotions love company, and they come in groups.

You get anxious about your goals, relationships, business, and specific situations. Even standing next to someone who triggers your insecurity might be a stressful event that throws you back into your dark corner, impacting your self-esteem and making you want to disappear on the spot.

Insecurity comes from instability and unpredictability. If adults are less affected by it, insecurity can affect children long-term. Children with an inconsistent parent may grow up anxious and fearful, not knowing what to expect from life just as they did not know what to expect from the parent, with that lack of any direction and vision for their life.

What It Does

To this wall, we often react by one of two extremes: we completely isolate ourselves from others, or we anxiously attach to someone or something. We also hold others and ourselves to perfectionism, when it is never good enough, and we make poor decisions. One good example is of a husband or wife who is insecure about themselves and will follow their spouse's every move, suspecting that anytime they do something or go somewhere, it is to be unfaithful.

Insecurity might push us to be better and evolve, or it may trap us in the corner of doing nothing with our lives besides pulling our hair out, not knowing what is next.

This feeling often resides in our hearts, and if it remains in our body and mind for too long, it may provoke physical disease, like obesity and related illnesses.

"Often those that criticize others reveal what he him-self lacks."—**Shannon L. Alder**

REJECTION

Did someone turn you down again? Maybe it happened in your relationship, career, or friendship, or maybe you are rejecting yourself?

Well do we remember those days in school when we were rejected by a group of students that we really wanted to be a part of or by our first love. Rejection is often more painful at a young age than when we get more years under our belts. (I hate to say getting older... I don't, I get wiser and more aware, and my body is on this planet for more years. The time will come when my vessel will have to go back to nature. Still, my energy lives forever because, if you remember, the law of conservation of energy states that energy can neither be created nor destroyed—only converted from one form of energy to another.) Sorry for my little detour about aging, but usually, if it comes when I write, that means it is meant to be here.

Rejection hurts. A lot. The reason is that we are meant to be social beings, and the acceptance of society is an essential part of our life. That is why centuries ago, one of the harshest punishments was exile. Scientists looked deeper by using MRIs to examine what is happening in our brain at the time of rejection, and it should come as no surprise that the same area of the brain that reacts to physical pain in the body is activated by the feeling of rejection as well.

Rejection can come in a few forms, and one could be more painful than another: rejection by someone or society, and self-rejection.

You could be rejecting yourself out of fear of being rejected by others. You keep hiding yourself in the wrong clothes, body, and emotions just to fit in with others. You keep saying NO to yourself and wearing a mask of someone else who you think will be more likely to be accepted by your close circle. That is the reason we often live in fear: that other people won't like the real us.

What It Does

According to the American Psychological Association:

"As researchers have dug deeper into the roots of rejection, they've found surprising evidence that the pain of being excluded is not so different from the pain of physical injury. Rejection also has serious implications for an individual's psychological state and for society in general."[38]

Social rejection increases anger, anxiety, depression, jealousy, and sadness. It reduces performance on difficult intellectual tasks and may also contribute to aggression and poor impulse control, as reviewed in "Social Acceptance and Rejection: The Sweet and the Bitter" by C. Nathan DeWall and Brad J. Bushman.[39]

Self-rejection might bring you to the realization later in life that you lived someone else's life and wore someone else's clothes and did someone else's job because all this time, you were saying NO to who you really are.

---

38 American Psychological Association. "The Pain of Social Rejection." Accessed July 31, 2023. https://www.apa.org/monitor/2012/04/rejection.
39 DeWall, C. Nathan, and Brad J. Bushman. "Social Acceptance and Rejection: The Sweet and the Bitter." *Current Directions in Psychological Science* 20, no. 4 (August 2011): 256–60. https://doi.org/10.1177/0963721411417545.

HATE

How often do you use the word hate? For real, every day in your regular life?

I hear people say: I hate this food, I hate when she says this, I hate when he does that, I hate working here, I hate doing this, I hate where I live, and so on. I mean, this word gets used a lot. I even hear people say: I hate my life.

I hope you believe that words have power, just as our thoughts and feelings do; otherwise, you wouldn't have picked up this book. We use it so often without genuinely meaning what we say or thinking about what we feel. What if every time we say it, there is a little bit more hate that gets expended into the world and into our life?

Hate has been described widely as an emotion, attitude, or sensation. A simple definition of hate is intense dislike, usually deriving from fear, anger, insecurity, or fear of injury. But for some reason, I believe it doesn't end there. Some describe hate as a blend of emotions such as anger, contempt, and disgust; others regard hate as a distinct and unique feeling.[40]

There are few studies about hate, why it is generated, and how. Here is what I found fascinating from one study:

"Hate seems most distinct from dislike and anger, somewhat less distinct from contempt, and least distinct from disgust. For instance, compared with dislike, anger or contempt (but not disgust), study participants rated their experiences of hate as more intense."[41]

So it is a very intense feeling, not like any other. Another study revealed that we mostly feel hate for people, groups, or situations if their

---

40 Psyche. "What Makes Hate a Unique Emotion – and Why That Matters | Psyche Ideas." Accessed July 31, 2023. https://psyche.co/ideas/what-makes-hate-a-unique-emotion-and-why-that-matters.
41 Martínez, C. A., van Prooijen, J.-W., & Van Lange, P. A. M. (2022). Hate: Toward understanding its distinctive features across interpersonal and intergroup targets. *Emotion, 22*(1), 46–63.

beliefs don't align with our belief of what is fair, noble, and right, or the idea of what is a good life or a good society.[42]

So if we hate something that doesn't feel fair, right, or noble, it could trigger us to make it right or to speak our truth. I don't remember when I ever hated anyone until the war began in Ukraine… I hate to see that one person can rule the minds and actions of millions to take what is not theirs and hate-kill thousands of people because of their desire for freedom.

I had to let go of hate and now remain in a state of love to both sides. You might disagree—I know most people in Ukraine would. But I prefer love over hate. We can't hold this feeling in our bodies for too long. It tenses every muscle and can drive us crazy, leading to unwarranted actions.

What It Does

Poison isn't always something you eat or drink—it can be an emotion. And hate is one of them, eating you up inside and causing destruction.[43]

I found the above phrase in the article "The Destructive Power of Hate" and thought I couldn't say it any better.

When you hate, instead of a state of creation, you enter a state of disruption. The disruption spreads in your body, mind, and the world around you. If you keep feeding hate with hateful thoughts, it will burn you down and spread. But recognizing it, becoming aware, and replacing it with understanding and love will help you to grow.

42 Psyche. "What Makes Hate a Unique Emotion – and Why That Matters | Psyche Ideas." Accessed July 31, 2023. https://psyche.co/ideas/what-makes-hate-a-unique-emotion-and-why-that-matters.
43 EverydayHealth.com. "The Destructive Power of Hate," July 26, 2023. https://www.everydayhealth.com/emotional-health/destructive-power-hate/.

HOPELESSNESS

"Hope can be a powerful force. Maybe there's no actual magic in it, but when you know what you hope for most and hold it like a light within you, you can make things happen, almost like magic."—**Laini Taylor**

If hope is a light that leads us even when it seems everything is going downhill, what is hopelessness? Is it complete darkness, or four walls with no exit door? It probably feels like a prison cell.

"Your life will be brighter than noonday; its darkness will be like the morning. You will be secure, because there is hope, and you will look around and lie down in safety."—**Job 11:17–19**

Hope is the last thing we hold on to when things are getting out of hand, and we have no control over anything. If there is hope, not everything is lost. But when we lose even this last light that might keep us moving and alive, what happens then?

I am crying while writing this because hopelessness is to me one of the most difficult emotions to experience. To tell you honestly, this book is not easy to write because I started with most walls that I deconstructed in my mind and my heart, but then I continued writing about another wall to realize that I never noticed it was there… but with an in-depth review and new understanding, it surfaced out from under dunes of sand that had buried it for months or even years.

We can experience hopelessness in many ways in different aspects of life: being forgotten or abandoned by others, lacking inspiration, feeling like there is nothing that can be done to help the situation, not feeling seen and heard, lacking freedom in some way, lacking the skills or resources to achieve what we want, lacking support when we need it. All of that and much more can feel like hopelessness. Some mental health conditions may also have hopelessness as one of the symptoms.

What I found interesting is that hopelessness is not solely an emotion. In addition to "negative" emotions like sorrow, despair, and fear, hopelessness includes pessimistic beliefs about the future. Beliefs are thoughts, not emotions.[44]

What It Does

Individuals with increased hopelessness have a greater risk of premature death, cancer, and heart disease.[45]

You probably already realized that all negative emotions greatly impact our physical and mental health, and as a result, our life, so I will not list all of that once again here but will share the art below.

44 The Berkeley Well-Being Institute. "Hopelessness: Definition, Examples, & Theory." Accessed July 31, 2023. https://www.berkeleywellbeing.com/hopelessness.html.
45 Everson, S. A., D. E. Goldberg, G. A. Kaplan, R. D. Cohen, E. Pukkala, J. Tuomilehto, and J. T. Salonen. "Hopelessness and Risk of Mortality and Incidence of Myocardial Infarction and Cancer." *Psychosomatic Medicine* 58, no. 2 (1996): 113–21. https://doi.org/10.1097/00006842-199603000-00003.

WORRY

You feel worried when you are constantly thinking about something that happened, which may be a signal that something bad will happen.[46]

We worry for so many reasons: exams are coming, the wedding is approaching, your boyfriend didn't call, your spouse didn't answer their phone, or you forgot the necessary paperwork at home that you need. I mean, we constantly have 100 reasons to worry.

Here is my rule about worrying: if it can be fixed, there is nothing to worry about; just go and fix it. If it can't be fixed, there is no reason to worry about it; give it to "hope," for example, or to "understanding" or to a higher power to figure things out.

But I know it's easy to worry, especially for mothers—we worry non-stop about everything.

Here is my story from years ago. I was pregnant with my son, and one day when I came home from work, my husband wasn't there. I called his phone a few times, but he didn't answer. I waited about 30 minutes and called more, probably at least 10 times. Here is the thing: on the way home, I had seen this horrible car crash… when my husband didn't answer, I thought to myself, *Something definitely happened.* I called his work and all his friends, but no one knew where he was. I panicked, cried, and prayed that everything was okay and that he was not in any accident. An hour later, one of his friends found him in a warehouse talking about work and cars with the business owner, and of course, there was no phone connection in the building. I thought in those two hours I would have a heart attack. I don't know where all that worry came from, but seeing that car crash on the way home had had more impact on me than I thought.

Why do we worry, and what is it? Worry is a type of fear we trigger by thinking ahead and anticipating the worst-case scenario. We have this

46 Wierzbicka, A. *Cognitive Domains and the Structure of the Lexicon: The Case of Emotions.* Vol. Mapping the mind: Domain specificity in cognition and culture. Cambridge University Press, 1994.

unique ability to imagine what may happen in the future. We use this ability sometimes not to our advantage, to think of what good can happen and
how we can plan upfront, but to fuel our own stress.

What It Does

When we fuel our own stress and negative emotions, the fight-or-
flight response kicks in, and because we do not actually fight or run away,
the worry piles up inside. Chronic worrying, anxiety, and more stress hor-
mones pour in with many unwanted consequences. I have listed them in
other chapters, so I will skip them here.

Here is a statistic to show that my rule works perfectly: "research
indicates that 85% of what subjects worried about did not actually happen,
and of the things that did happen, 79% was manageable."[47]

---

47 "'Worry' Is a Useless Emotion! | Psychology Today." Accessed July 31, 2023. https://www.
psychologytoday.com/us/blog/the-high-functioning-alcoholic/201906/worry-is-useless-emotion.

ANXIETY

The perfect place for anxiety is between worry and fear. I feel just this one sentence explains what anxiety is. So if fear is one of the basic emotions, anxiety is a state of mind or mood. Just like worry, anxiety is a feeling of unease about a future threat, a threat you might not even be able to name, and are not sure where it is coming from or if it is coming at all.

Approximately 19% of adults in the United States struggle with anxiety every day.[48]

When your inner protector is always on the lookout for dangerous situations, your body and mind are tense, waiting, and preparing to run or fight. Occasional anxiety is okay, and just like any other negative emotion, it is there for a reason. But anxiety disorders are different: "They're a group of mental illnesses that cause constant and overwhelming anxiety and fear. Excessive anxiety can make you avoid work, school, family get-togethers, and other social situations."[49]

What It Does

I hear about this feeling from my clients a lot. At least once every few sessions, I have a client who would say they felt anxious. If you felt that at least once in your lifetime, you would not forget. I remember times when I felt anxious, I was dizzy, I had trouble sleeping, my stomach quit on me, and my heart rate went up and stayed higher than usual. Sound familiar? Your symptoms might be different, but feeling nervous, restless, or tense; having a sense of doom or a ringing in your ears; sweating, trouble concentrating, and feeling insecure are all symptoms of anxiety.

---

48 "Anxiety: What You Need To Know | McLean Hospital." Accessed July 31, 2023. https://www.mcleanhospital.org/essential/anxiety.
49 Contributors, WebMD Editorial. "All About Anxiety Disorders: From Causes to Treatment and Prevention." WebMD. Accessed July 31, 2023. https://www.webmd.com/anxiety-panic/anxiety-disorders.

Anxiety disorders have a greater effect on your body and mind. Some are characterized by chest pains, panic attacks, heart attacks, and even choking. From my experience, I think our anxiety gets created in our stomach. That is why we either feel no appetite or try to eat more than we need to absorb the anxiety.

> *"Worrying about outcomes over which I have no control is punishing myself before the universe has decided whether I ought to be punished."*—**Sherry Thomas, A Study in Scarlet Women**

CONTEMPT

The baseline for contempt is when we think: "I'm better than you, and you are lesser than me." Synonyms of contempt are scorn, disdain, and disrespect. Usually based on moral views and personal standards, it is the feeling that somehow we are better than another person or a group of people. We may feel judgemental and disgusted together with contempt.

"Nothing living should ever be treated with contempt. Whatever it is that lives, a man, a tree, or a bird, should be touched gently, because the time is short. Civilization is another word for respect for life..." **Elizabeth Goudge, Green Dolphin Street**

We are all here for a reason, and we are trying to live the best life we possibly can.

This was one of the reasons I left Ukraine years ago. I think I had this wall in my mind built by Ukrainian society, but it was destroyed when I moved to the United States. I hope it has changed with the years, but my family seemed surprised that here people are less contemptuous than where I am from.

Here is why: in Ukraine, it is okay to be a waitress till you are about 20 years old. If you are still a waitress after that, people will look at you and think that somehow you are a little bit stupid and could not get a better job. It is related to housekeeping, babysitting, any type of cleaner, anybody who deals with garbage disposal, and many other jobs. People with a higher professional status would look down on those who do service jobs. It's sad, I know. Here I love that it doesn't matter where you work and what you do. You are important to society by serving in any capacity. My sister had to work as a housekeeper when she came here as a refugee, and she felt awful about that because of what she remembered and believed about doing this type of job in my country.

The situation I described is one of the reasons why someone may feel contempt. There are many reasons why one could feel they are somehow better than others:

"People who genuinely believe that everyone is equal will most likely not feel contempt towards others. However, most social structures have a hierarchical classification of some sort, because it functions to reward people who exhibit praiseworthy behavior and punish people who behave poorly. People who feel contempt have an urge to disassociate from the target, for instance, by avoiding them, ignoring them, or banning them from the social group."[50]

I prefer empathy, compassion, and understanding over contempt. But again, contempt is not always bad. If this feeling can help you to see an abusive relationship, for example, and give you that first reason to get out of it, your contempt serves you well.

What It Does

This emotion may harm others around you, but it can also harm you. You might start to isolate yourself from society and, as a result, become depressed. Remember, each of the emotions I am talking about is okay in short doses but unhealthy in the long run.

In this chapter, I will do what I didn't for any of the other emotional walls because I think this emotion is the easiest to overcome.

You can start by saying something like:

We are all humans. No one is better than anyone else, and we are all on our personal journey to learn something.

Ask yourself these questions:

What if someone looked down on me the same way I look down on someone else? How would I feel?

What if I could wear glasses of empathy and compassion? What would change?

50 Emotion Typology. "Contempt." Accessed July 31, 2023. https://emotiontypology.com/negative_emotion/contempt/.

How can I show compassion?

DESPERATION

"When you reach the end of your rope, tie a knot and hang on."—
Abraham Lincoln

"You seem very desperate to get married."

"No, I am not. I just really want to have a husband with all my heart and have been running around trying to find one," I was once told.

We might face desperation when we really want to achieve something (or don't want something to happen), and we do all we can, but it doesn't look or feel like success awaits us.

Desperation and determination seem to stand very close to each other. However, desperation produces a negative vibe—the vibe of neediness, not the vibe of being set in your purpose or resolute about something. And by running on the negative frequency of desperation, we get absolutely nowhere.

People can usually sense our neediness and don't want to participate. That is why some businesses can't lift off the ground: because the owner is working from the vibration of desperation and neediness.

According to Emotion Typology, "People in desperation are often willing and able to do things they would otherwise not consider, such as breaking the law or begging for help, depending on the importance of the goal."[51]

I am sure you have seen this before. In this state of mind and the signals we send to our body and to the world, we usually can't get the outcome we want. It seems as if we are running like a hamster on a wheel, and everyone sees that we need to get off to grab that nut a foot away, but no one really cares.

---

51 Emotion Typology. "Desperation." Accessed July 31, 2023. https://emotiontypology.com/negative_emotion/desperation/.

Desperation is not entirely an emotion or feeling. It mostly lives in our heads and is fueled by our thoughts and beliefs, sometimes due to social standards.

What It Does

Desperation can burn you out mentally and physically. You will feel like you have tried everything, but nothing helps. Desperation will keep you stressed, and eventually, you might start experiencing all the side effects of it.

Let go, and believe that the right things will happen on their own when they need to.

SADNESS

We all know sadness. We get to know this emotion from a young age. We felt sad when we didn't get that puppy for our birthday, when our friend went to play with someone else on the playground, and when Daddy was deployed for six months. We continue to feel this emotion through adulthood.

We often say we feel sad if we can't quite put our finger on what is wrong, but we know we are not happy. We feel sad when we lose something that was important to us. It can be a person, a material thing, a pet, an opportunity, an activity, or even a feeling we had before.

Sadness is not an exception, and it likes to show up with disappointment, anger, or pity, or as a supporter of other negative emotions like grief, loneliness, helplessness, and others.

Researchers didn't know what this emotion was for or what it signaled for a long time, but now researchers believe that sadness acts as a mild alert, as though calling for help from others to recoup and regroup.

A few weeks ago, I sat down to watch a cartoon with my son. We looked together and found *Inside Out*, an Academy Award-winning movie about Riley's emotions. When I watched it, I thought to myself, *This is genius. I am writing this part in the book about negative emotions, and in this movie, I get to see how we each have four negative emotions and one positive emotion: Joy.* Joy tries to control Riley every day and put more joy in Riley's life as she grows. If everyone understands what anger, fear, and disgust are there for, no one understands the purpose of sadness. When Joy gets lost in Riley's long-term memory, she realizes that Sadness does play a significant role for survival. According to Khiron Clinics:

"Sadness emphasizes other feelings, such as compassion, empathy, or love, and it connects people on a deeper level. Sadness is not just about being sad. Visible sadness in one person can evoke empathy and acquire support from others, strengthening social bonds."[52]

If you didn't watch that cartoon, do. It is a fun one. I had an aha moment that I will tell you about in the last chapter of this part.

Sadness is a normal emotion, and you should experience it from time to time as long as you don't get stuck in it. Otherwise, you will be facing depression with a more negative impact on your life.

When feeling sad, you still should be able to go about your day-to-day activities, but depression might hold you in a bad mood all day long or maybe even a week or more.

What It Does

As we said, sadness is not as bad as we think. It is there to help us, but if you feel sad for prolonged periods, you might be depressed, and that can be destructive to your relationships, work, and health. Depression can

52 Araminta. "Exploring Emotion: Sadness." *Khiron Clinics* (blog), May 22, 2020. https:// khironclinics.com/blog/exploring-emotion-sadness/.

increase pain in several body parts and lead to chronic pain without obvious physical traumas.

Sadness grows in our lungs, so you might find your breathing is shallow, and inhaling a full chest of air seems challenging.

Here is another insight that came to me: depression can increase your risk for colon cancer. That might be why we see a rise in this type of cancer because we see a rise in depression among people in the United States.

GREED

I was uncertain about this chapter, asking myself if greed is a feeling or an emotion, or a behavior triggered by other feelings and emotions.

What do you think?

I know we often think of greed as a characteristic of someone's personality, but here is my conclusion: if desire is a feeling (psychologists argue about this as well), then a strong desire to own something, a lot of something, is also a feeling.

What does greed look like? It is an extreme desire, a burning need to possess something. *Psychology Today*, in a few articles, mentions that greed is like an addiction. Greed, just like any other addiction, fires up the same areas of the brain, signaling to us that enough is never enough. Usually, we think of a greedy person in relation to material things and money. A person who would never spend any extra and do everything to accumulate more, even through harming others, is said to be greedy.

Maybe you thought for a moment here, *What if I want to make more money? Am I greedy?* Not necessarily. To want more is normal and drives us to grow and evolve. Usually, we start with wanting money to provide for our basic needs, and then we might move to wanting more knowledge, understanding, or service to others. At least, this is the healthy way to want more.

But greediness, on the other hand, is driven by negative vibrations in our bodies and surroundings. Often a greedy person tries to fill some internal void by possessing more and holding on to everything he gets his hands on.

Writing about that, I thought of hoarding. Is it from greed? Perhaps, but it could also be because of a mental disorder.

Here is why I decided to include this here: greed often comes with other negative emotions such as desperation, jealousy, envy, stress, neediness, stress, and depression. That is why we read much about *not* being greedy in the Bible.

"Watch out! Be on your guard against all kinds of greed; a man's life does not consist in the abundance of his possessions."—**Luke 12:15**

What It Does

It is not as strong as other emotions, but when experiencing greed, you are always in a state of stress in order to gain more or hold on to something you don't need but are unwilling to share with others or simply to throw it away.

With constant stress, you will have similar risks to your health as with other emotions we talked about.

And here is why I used this illustration when I was writing this chapter: I looked to my window to see a swift sitting on my blinds inside the house. I was surprised and could not understand how it got in, but I thought it might be a sign. Maybe you can find a meaning as to why it is here in this specific place of the book. We did rescue the bird, by the way, and let it out. No worries, my cat didn't eat it.

EMOTIONAL OVERWHELM

We are coming to the last few chapters in this part of the book, and we have looked at many negative emotions and feelings as walls. I should include the one I hear my clients use the most: overwhelm. Every client shared that they felt overwhelmed at one point or another. I decided to look a little bit deeper into the meeting of feeling overwhelmed. Apparently, it is not a specific feeling or emotion. According to *Good Therapy*, "Emotional overwhelm occurs when the intensity of your feelings outmatches your ability to manage them. An individual is most likely to be overwhelmed by negative emotions like anger, fear, or guilt."[53]

And you may wonder, is it good to be overwhelmed by positive emotions? I don't think being overwhelmed is used toward positive emotions a lot. However, people experiencing mania can be overwhelmed by euphoria.

When we think of being overwhelmed, we usually think of being under the stress of having a lot on our shoulders. Often, we use overwhelmed to describe how we feel in the moment.

Sometimes it could be challenging to identify what exactly made you feel that way, and it doesn't have to be a significant stressor. It could be a pile of small things dumped on you unexpectedly.

Being under that weight can make you overreact to other things in your everyday life, like your child spilling some water on the floor. Your mind might be foggy, and you might have trouble focusing on important tasks or even simple things.

What It Does

Good Therapy goes on to state:

---

53 "Emotional Overwhelm." Accessed July 31, 2023. https://www.goodtherapy.org/learn-about-therapy/issues/emotional-overwhelm.

"Emotional overwhelm can make it difficult to take care of yourself. You may forget meals, skip rest breaks, or struggle to fall asleep. These behaviors can in turn lower your ability to think rationally, making it even harder to cope with overwhelm."[54]

Emotional overwhelm can make you feel ill and lower your energy levels. Being in a prolonged state of overwhelm can lead to depression and overeating.

---

54 "Emotional Overwhelm." Accessed July 31, 2023. https://www.goodtherapy.org/learn-about-therapy/issues/emotional-overwhelm.

FEAR

It is familiar to everyone, the queen of all negative emotions and a shield from danger: fear itself.

All negative emotions take root from this one. I believe we have two fundamental feelings that birth the rest: all positive feelings and emotions come from love, and all negative ones come from fear. Those two are basics, and we all carry them in our DNA.

> *"And above all these put on love, which binds every-thing together in perfect harmony."*—**Colossians 3:14**

However, here is what I believe to be true. I think our soul doesn't have fear; beyond our material world, fear doesn't exist. We carry the knowledge of fear, but it doesn't wake up by itself.

> *"For God gave us a spirit not of fear but of power and love and self-control."*—**Timothy 1:7**

Here is why. If you pay attention to your children or grandchildren, when we start to explore the world, we are fearless but very curious.

I imagine a child's mind while exploring: *What are those two holes in the wall? What do they do? What a beautiful creature. Can I touch it? Water, I love water!* A mother's duty, with all her learned fear, is to keep her child alive. If in prehistoric times our fear was for our children to get eaten by predators, nowadays it is to get electrocuted.

Did you pay attention to how a child learns to be afraid? If the mother, or more rarely, the father, runs towards the child, scared and with big, open eyes, screaming "NOOOO!" that means the child shouldn't touch it or should get away from it.

Fear is learned from others; it is conditioned fear. And then there is our own learned fear. We do something that hurts or is unpleasant in some way or makes us feel insecure. We learn not to do it again, and we remember it with the same feeling of fear. It is an amazing software installed in us and in most creatures on Earth to keep us alive. Every negative emotion has its place and must coexist with all the positive ones out there. If the Divine or God's creation is perfect with no mistakes or faults, then our fear software is no mistake, together with all the updates and additions.

But if we live in permanent fear, sometimes even not understanding where we got it from, we are not living; we are surviving. We are just keeping ourselves alive without any joy or drive to truly live. In that state of mind, we are paralyzed and dead inside.

What It Does

Fear is a big topic in psychology. According to *Very Well*:

"Many types of fear exist, including phobias, agoraphobia, generalized anxiety disorder, panic disorder, post-traumatic stress disorder (PTSD), separation anxiety disorder, and social anxiety disorder."[55]

The body's reaction to occasional fear is the same as to many other negative feelings: the fight-or-flight response. By the way, it is improved now: psychologists refer to the "fight, flight, or freeze" response with all the ingredients of sweating, increased heart rate, and high adrenaline levels. But consistent fear will keep your mind and body stressed all the time.

---

55 Verywell Mind. "The Psychology of Fear." Accessed July 31, 2023. https://www.verywellmind.com/the-psychology-of-fear-2671696.

HOW TO CRACK WALLS OF EMOTIONS AND FEELINGS

"Everything that happens to us emotionally or psychologically happens to our bodies as well. It's all connected." —**James S. Gordon, MD**

You might think you are finally going to read about how to deal with all of your trapped emotions. But first, let's find out why some emotions get trapped. Should we have a built-in mechanism for how to deal with and process negative emotions?

And you are right. Mother nature and the Divine are brilliant, and they did put that mechanism in every one of us, but with time, we break it, and for some of us, it stops working.

There are two types of emotions and feelings:

What we experience in the moment; and

Information and energy (emotions) stored in our body from past experiences.

Here is the natural way to process emotions: rest–alert–fight/flight/freeze–experience emotion–return to safety–rest and digest.

One of the most important stages that we decided to control and change is the "experience emotion" stage. When our body tries to return to calm by physically going through emotions, it can release the adrenaline and burn off the stress. And you probably know how that happens: we cry, scream, and laugh hysterically sometimes, all to release unneeded chemicals in our body and return to the rest state.

But I remember really clearly that my parents always told me: "No need to cry," "People will laugh if you do," "Pretty girls don't cry," "No one likes crying babies," and so on. You probably heard something similar in your childhood. So we started to believe that and resist any negative emotion going through us and hold it together or hold it in so no one would see us crying, screaming, or falling apart.

And what if everything is energy—including the negative emotion that is going through you right now like a wave? What happens when you resist and hold it in, put a lock on it, and keep it together so no one can say, "Something is wrong with her. Why is she crying?"

By resisting or holding it in, it doesn't matter if you look from a chemical or energy perspective. You trap that negative emotion inside your body. It goes and finds the weakest spot to reside inside.

Mark Olson, PhD, LMT, says:

"The phrase 'trapped emotions' usually means that the true self wants to express something that the false self doesn't want us to express. In psychology, we think of the true self as the part of us that we are born with that is naturally open, curious, and trusting, while the false self emerges as a set of adaptive strategies to deal with pain and loss."[56]

---

56 Healthline. "Are You Carrying 'Emotional Baggage' Here's How to Break Free," September 16, 2021. https://www.healthline.com/health/mind-body/how-to-release-emotional-baggage-and-the-tension-that-goes-with-it.

Have you heard of Dr. Masaru Emoto's experiments with water? His book *The Messages Of Water* showed that our thoughts and emotions change how water crystallizes. I would put it differently: how positive and negative energy influence water molecules. And if energy profoundly influences water molecules, don't you think it affects any molecule it interacts with? But even if we stick with water for the sake of argument, you probably remember from school that our body is 60% water, our brain is 85% water, and our heart is 79% water, even if we don't see it with the naked eye.

I know; we think we are not liquid. We are really solid beings. But nevertheless, it is a fact, and if energy waves can impact how water behaves, negative emotions will start affecting the part of the body where they got trapped and, if not cleared, can create illness and organ malfunction.

Here is another crazy thing you might ask me: why did I take time to explore 25 negative emotions? If an emotion is trapped, it is trapped, and similar techniques are used to release it.

There are more than 25 negative emotions. I gave you a list of the most common ones. The more you are aware and understand what you are dealing with, the easier it will be to work through it.

Every emotion has a different energy wave, and not only that, every negative emotion has it is own unique heartbeat rhythm.

After understanding how important it is to go through the entire cycle to process the emotion we are experiencing, we can finally let go at those moments, cry, scream, and do what it takes not to end up with that trapped emotion.

Reading Michael A. Singer, *The Untethered Soul: The Journey Beyond Yourself*, I thought I could not say it better than this:

"When you feel pain [he talks about different negative emotions here], simply view it as energy. Just start seeing these inner experiences as energy passing through your heart and before the eye of your consciousness. Then relax. Do the opposite of contracting and closing. Relax and release. Relax your heart until you are actually face-to-face with the exact place where it hurts. Stay open and receptive so you can be present right where the tension is. You must be willing to be present right at the place of the tightness and pain, and then relax and go even deeper. This is very deep growth and transformation. But you will not want to do this. You will feel tremendous resistance to doing this, and that's what makes it so powerful. As you relax and feel the resistance, the heart will want to pull away, to close, to protect, and to defend itself. Keep relaxing. Relax your shoulders and relax your heart. Let go and give room for the pain to pass through you. It's just energy. Just see it as energy and let it go."[57]

But there is not a lot we can do about information stored in our body from previous experiences, and those can influence our health and how we feel, act, and behave. According to Business Day:

"A Harvard School of Public Health study showed people who bottled up their emotions increased their chance of premature death from all causes by more than 30%, with their risk of being diagnosed with cancer increasing by 70%. Unexpressed and unacknowledged emotions are the cause of 85% of diseases. When your buried emotions are not expressed or recognized, they will always find a way to show up and show out. Your emotional energy is always trying to be heard and expressed in some way. If you do not recognize your emotions for what they are and find healthy ways to express them, they "will" find a way to express themselves anyway."[58]

I know this might be a weird thing to hear from me... because I always used to say, "Mindset, mindset, and more mindset can fix our life." Here, I will offer different approaches from several books that I think say something similar. These are from doctors and healers who came to new solutions and have been helping many people.

I researched many articles and books, but I picked these five to show you the similarities I found among them:

Feelings Buried Alive Never Die by Karol K. Truman

The Emotion Code: How to Release Your Trapped Emotions for Abundant Health, Love, and Happiness by Dr. Bradley Nelson

57 Singer, Michael A. *The Untethered Soul: The Journey beyond Yourself.* Oakland, CA: New Harbinger Publications, 2007.
58 BusinessDay. "How Painful Emotions Buried Alive Never Die." Businessday NG, January 20, 2023. https://businessday.ng/news/article/how-painful-emotions-buried-alive-never-die/.

The Untethered Soul: The Journey Beyond Yourself by Michael A. Singer

The Power of Infinite Love & Gratitude: An Evolutionary Journey to Awakening Your Spirit by Darren R. Weissman

You Are the Placebo: Making Your Mind Matter by Joe Dispenza

I found that all of them talk about our trapped emotions in some way, and each of these books offers a way to release them. Some use prayer to find and release emotion, some use meditation, others use muscle testing to ask your body to find it and use feelings of love and gratitude or magnets to remove it.

I think they all work as long as you believe in them and do it intentionally. My favorite that I tried is *The Emotion Code*. I use it for myself. It is available for everyone out there.

Each of these approaches uses:

- **Awareness**
- **Intention**
- **Love and gratitude**
- **Connection with the Divine**
- **Forgiveness and letting go**

You can use one of the methods these books offer, or you can come up with your own with the above ingredients, and I have no doubt that it will work.

As I said, I believe that there are two main emotions: fear (and all negative emotions come from fear) and love (and all positive emotions come from some form of love). If our trapped negative emotions can become poison, infinite and unconditional love through all its forms can become a cure.

"Do everything in love."—***Corinthians 16:14***

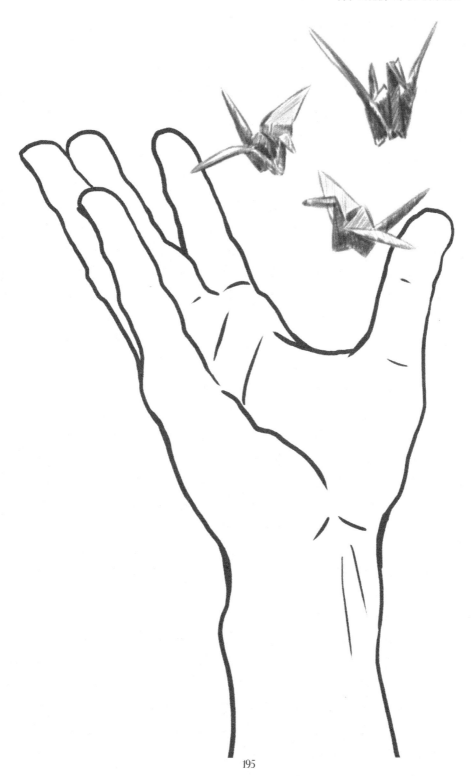

Part IV: Other Walls

Welcome to Part IV, and congratulations because you are already aware of 75 different walls that can stop you from being your own success story. These are 75 walls that can build your own prison that feels impossible to escape.

So we are at our last 25 walls, and I called them "Other Walls" because they are not "I Walls," "They Walls," or "Feelings Walls"... These are other walls that were built by society and passed from generation to generation. They are often untrue or don't serve us in our modern age. But nevertheless, we stick to them and continue to pass them to our children because, oh well, that is what we were taught. So "Other Walls" are walls of social statements and assumptions, sometimes put in idioms that are easy to remember and that we all know.

Expressions and idioms are important components of any language. Each culture has its unique and special phrases. In my country, we have idioms that are hard to explain here, and my parents and grandparents have told me many of them over the years. For instance, the saying "Don't run before the train" means not to do things before it is necessary.

Idioms and well-known social statements are frequently used to convey a particular idea or feeling. However, they can also limit our success in certain circumstances and affect our decision-making. They are just more walls built in our brain by multiple repetitions that make us believe something or not believe in it.

For example, the saying "The apple doesn't fall far from the tree" insinuates that an individual will inevitably adopt the same habits and behaviors as their parents, often with a negative connotation. This will be discussed in detail in one of the upcoming chapters. If we take this saying to heart, we may be less inclined to believe that we have control over our own future and may subject ourselves to a life similar to our parents', even if we do not desire it.

Idioms can also hinder our progress by promoting conformity to societal norms or expectations. For instance, the phrase "go along to get along" suggests that it is preferable to blend in with the crowd rather than stand out or challenge the status quo. If we consistently adhere to this advice, we may miss out on opportunities to create positive changes or innovate in our personal lives or communities.

It's important to understand that a lot of statements we were told as children are misleading or untrue, causing us to make poor choices or miss out on opportunities. Take the phrase "Money can't buy happiness," a favorite I used as one big limiting belief in one of my money-mindset workshops. I even dug out scientific proof that is not true anymore, which I will share with you in the chapter about it as well.

So let's start breaking those stereotypical sayings we heard numerous times, which can possibly limit our mindset to not get what we came here for.

LIFE IS HARD/THIS IS JUST THE WAY IT IS

*"Problems are not stop signs, they are guidelines."—**Robert Schuller***

Ethologist John B. Calhoun conducted experiments on rats and mice. He created mice and rat utopias to provide everything they needed to grow the population. But nevertheless, in every experiment, the population stopped growing after hitting a certain number, even still having space and everything else it needed to grow. However:

"In his most famous experiment in the series, Universe 25, the population peaked at 2,200 mice and thereafter exhibited a variety of abnormal, often destructive, behaviors, including refusal to engage in courtship, females abandoning their young, and males who only cared for their appearance. By the 600th day, the population was on its way to extinction. Though physically able to reproduce, the mice had lost the social skills required to mate."[59]

Reading about this experiment made me think about what is happening in the world now. We have everything we ever will need (in the US) and less and less hardship. But for some reason, there are more mental health issues, fewer marriages, and more people who are choosing not to have children. I am not criticizing or judging anyone. But these phenomena remind me of the Universe 25 experiment.

Why am I telling you about it here? Life gets hard sometimes, no doubt, but that is itself a reason to push through, grow, and continue our population because if life stops being hard at all, we might get depressed and stop socializing. I know it sounds like a big paradox... but life's problems

---

59 "Behavioral Sink." In *Wikipedia*, June 25, 2023. https://en.wikipedia.org/w/index.php?title=Behavioral_sink&oldid=1161835346.

drive us to invent, develop, and even write books. Most nonfiction books were written to solve some type of problem for their readers.

No problems, and life will get boring.

So embrace problems and challenges because something beautiful is usually born out of hardship and pressure, just like diamonds.

Why It Happens

I think we are brought here to learn, and sometimes the lessons are taught through difficult situations and problems in our life. But there is always light, and there is always an exit. The faster you learn your lessons, the faster they will pass through your life.

How To Crack This Wall

Start looking for your lessons. Why are you in this or that situation, and what is it trying to teach you?

My life hasn't been easy since the day I was born. I faced a lot of problems and moments I thought I wouldn't find an exit from. But everyone taught me a lesson I needed to help myself and others and even to write my first book.

You can start by saying something like:

I can see my lesson, and I am ready to learn it.

Ask yourself these questions:

What is my situation trying to teach me?

What are the positives?

How am I learning my lesson?

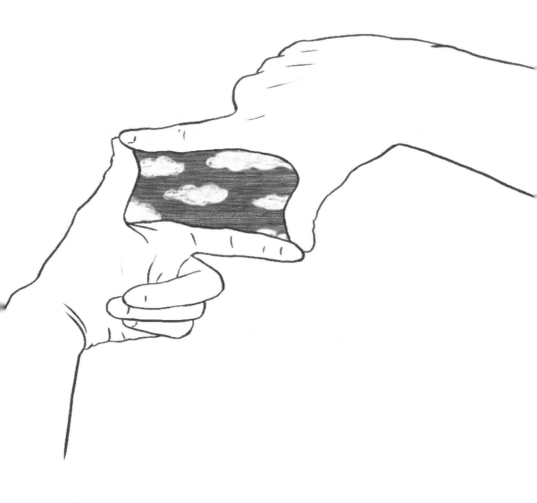

THERE ARE NOT ENOUGH OPPORTUNITIES

Who still believes this? Is it you? Really? Just like the thought that there are not enough ideas, creativity, or money to go around, this is also a myth.

In my previous book, I gave you this theory: if an idea is looking to be yours, it will knock on your door for some time, but if you don't do anything about it, it will go elsewhere. Or it might show up to a few people simultaneously, waiting for its birth in the material world.

Opportunities are no different. They will show up and wait around for you to claim, sometimes only for a short while, but if you don't, they will go elsewhere. The same opportunity may even show up to a few people at once, so you need to be open enough to see it and act on it.

Opportunities are almost like butterfly pets; they need an owner as soon as possible and don't live for long. They come and go, which is why they are so beautiful and desirable.

But of course, if you go around complaining that there are no opportunities, guess what you will attract? You get what you focus on. So start turning your attention to *There are opportunities everywhere, I am just waiting to grab one when it gets close, and I definitely will see and recognize it for what it is.*

Why It Happens

When we concentrate on negative things, or a lack of positive things, our brain gets programmed to look for proof of our thoughts, including the lack of what we want or desire. But if you switch your thoughts and start looking for possibilities and opportunities, everything will change.

How To Crack This Wall

While fighting one of my limiting beliefs about money, I decided to do a small experiment. I will tell you more about it in the chapter about money. But I want to share here what I discovered: when I turned my attention to seeing only money that showed up easily, I started to see money everywhere.

You can start by saying something like:

Opportunities are everywhere, and I am open to seeing and accepting them.

Ask yourself these questions:

What if there are many opportunities?

Do I need to focus on abundance instead of lack?

What can I do in the next few days to shift my attention in the right direction?

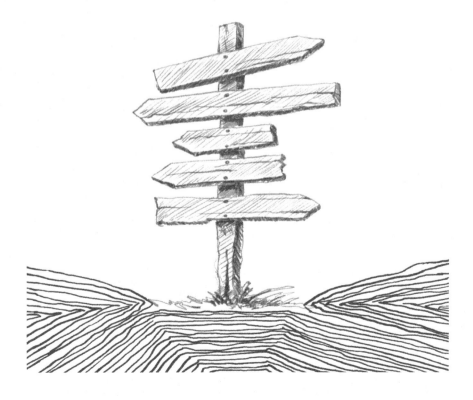

IT IS WHAT IT IS. JUST ACCEPT IT.

This phrase is often used for situations we can't control, and often we do just need to accept our circumstances to be able to move forward.

But be honest, how often do you use this phrase for a situation within your control?

Okay, let's review for a second what you can't control and what you can. And for that first part, I will totally say, "Just accept it and let it go."

Things we can't control:

Other people's actions

Other people's feelings

Other people's beliefs

Other people's thoughts

Let's stop here for a second and summarize anything regarding other people you can't control, even if they are your family members or best friends. Here you might think, *What about my young children? I can control them*, and I'm afraid I must again disagree. You can influence and lead by example, but forget about control.

More things we can't control:

The past

The future

The exact outcome of anything

Change

The weather

Traffic

And cats, let's not forget them. (I have a cat, so I can confirm.)

This is just a small, simple list. Now here is the important part…

Things you can control: **Yourself! And everything about yourself!**

Including:

How you talk to yourself

How you talk to others

What meals you eat, and how often

What you think of yourself and others

What emotions and feelings you choose to hold on to

How often you pick up your phone to scroll through social media

How often you call your friends and family

Whom you follow, the websites you visit, the blogs you read

What books you read

How often you watch TV

Your schedule

Your productivity

Your priorities

I mean, the list is long, but remember that the only thing in your control is you and only you.

So why do we so often think things in our control are not worth the fight, and we just bang ourselves against the wall with, "It is what it is. Just accept it"?

Why It Happens

We use this as a cover for taking responsibility. Accepting things as they are can lead to feelings of resignation and passivity. It can also create an obstacle to positive change and growth. This thinking may even normalize negative situations or behaviors, making individuals more likely to tolerate unhealthy or harmful conditions rather than seeking solutions or making necessary changes.

How To Crack This Wall

So next time someone tells you, or you tell yourself, "It is what it is, just accept it," respond by saying something like:

I can control everything within me and how I influence the world around me.

Ask yourself these questions:

What makes me think this situation is out of my control?

What can I control in this situation?

How can my actions influence this situation?

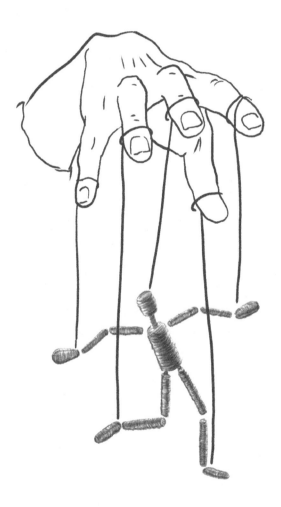

YOU HAVE TO WORK HARD TO MAKE MONEY

In 2020, I worked for a company as a Community Association Manager, making decent money. But after having my baby, I could not be there for 40 hours per week as before. However, I was still able to perform the same responsibilities. So my manager offered me a deal. He said, "How about we change your location, and you will only work 20 hours per week?" I agreed right away. But then he continued, "We will have to cut your pay by about $10K." At first, I thought, *Well, maybe it is not too bad for a new mother.*

I had about a month to think about it. During that month, several questions arose, and I heard a few phrases that changed my life and my perception of how much I could make at any given time.

I was told:

"It is acceptable for a woman to make less money after having a baby, and working less or not at all is okay."

But, acceptable for WHOM? And why should that be acceptable? Don't we need *more* money, not less, to support another human being?

I feel it is acceptable if it is the mother's decision, but not someone else's.

Through all the questions that came up in my mind, I knew I was cheaping out on myself right then and there. Why could I not work less *and* make more?

Then it hit me, and I realized:

I can make exactly as much as I think I can make, and it doesn't have to be hard.

This realization was a turning point for me. I learned that my earning potential is not limited to what other people think I'm capable of or even what I think of myself, and it doesn't have to be a complicated process.

Why It Happens

Do you want it or not? We still live by a lot of stereotypes. One of those is that you have to work hard and often to make money.

Well, what I learned is that not all hard work pays well. A lot of jobs involving physical work are hard and challenging, but they don't pay the best dollar for your sweat and your time.

Working smart, not hard, is the most effective way to earn money, and the 80/20 rule, also known as the Pareto Principle, supports this idea. Essentially, this principle states that 20% of your activities produce 80% of your results. To make the most of this rule, you must identify the top 20% of your actions or tasks that yield the most success. This principle can be applied to both your professional and personal life.[60]

How To Crack This Wall

You can start by saying something like:

---

60 "Pareto Principle." In *Wikipedia*, July 31, 2023. https://en.wikipedia.org/w/index.php?title=Pareto_principle&oldid=1168013778.

I can make exactly as much as I think I can make, and it doesn't have to be hard.

Ask yourself these questions:

What effective ways can I earn money at this time of my life?

What strategies have other people used to make money the easy way, and how can I apply them too?

What 20% of my activities produce 80% of my results (money)?

CHANGE IS TOO HARD

In one of his tweets, *Tony Robbins* wrote—*"Change is automatic. Progress is not. Progress is the result of conscious thought, decision, and action."*

So if change is automatic, why do many of us usually meet change with closed doors hoping it won't come to our house?

We all experience change, sometimes forced and sometimes voluntary. But why is it so difficult to change how we act, behave, and choose even if we know it is for the best? And probably from making new year's resolutions, like eating healthy and exercising daily, you learned that positive change is difficult.

The University of Chicago gives us more information:

"Did you know that your brain is made up of approximately 100 billion neurons, also known as brain cells? These neurons have the remarkable capacity to store and transmit vast amounts of information. Every time you acquire new knowledge or engage in a new activity, these neurons modify their connections with other neurons, allowing you to learn and grow."[61]

As you learn to drive a car, for example, you acquire new knowledge about the vehicle and its functions. You become familiar with the physical movements required to operate it, such as accelerating, braking, and reversing. Furthermore, you learn to interpret and respond to your surroundings, recognizing that a red light signifies to stop, and a green light indicates to proceed. In addition, if a pedestrian unexpectedly crosses the road, you must come to a halt. Each piece of information activates different areas of the brain and neurons. Repeated activation of these patterns leads to the formation of new neural connections, resulting in the creation of a new pathway.

---

61 "Neuroscientist Leads Unprecedented Research to Map Billions of Brain Cells." Accessed July 31, 2023. https://www.uchicagomedicine.org/forefront/neurosciences-articles/can-100-billion-neurons-be-mapped.

Why It Happens

Have you ever noticed how driving becomes almost effortless after you've done it for a while? It's like your brain has created a "car driving" pathway that strengthens with practice. The first time you drive, this pathway is weak, so you may sweat and focus intensely. However, with repetition, your brain becomes so accustomed to the process that you can drive without much concentration. This can sometimes lead to absentmindedness. If we get on the same road that we drive daily to work, but we had intended to stop at the store or see a friend, we pass the turn and only after a minute realize our mistake. Has this ever happened to you? No worries because I thought I was a weirdo with a bad memory on the road. I am glad I am not alone.

The same happens with our habits, behaviors, and choices. Every time we try to change a habit, we inevitably encounter resistance. This is due to our brain's preference for familiar pathways, as it always seeks the easiest route. When we deviate from these habitual patterns, our brain expends more energy, causing us to tire more rapidly. Moreover, if we become fatigued or stressed, our brain will relinquish conscious control, leading us to revert to our past habits or pathways.

So change is difficult for our brain because it literally needs to rewire itself to support a new habit or new behavior or simply to do something in a new way.

Change is not complicated, but it is a conscious choice that pushes your brain to make new connections.

How To Crack This Wall

First, understand change is happening in the world around you, whether you like it or not. But it is your choice to stick to old beliefs and old ways or to move together and change too.

Everything in the world is changing. Look at nature: once there is no more change, there is no more life. Stop holding on to the idea that the wheel doesn't need to be reinvented if it is working. What if it only works at 20% of its capacity, and you can improve it?

You can start by saying something like:

Change is part of life.

Ask yourself these questions:

What would I like to change in my life?

How can change help me?

What pattern in my brain would I want to change?

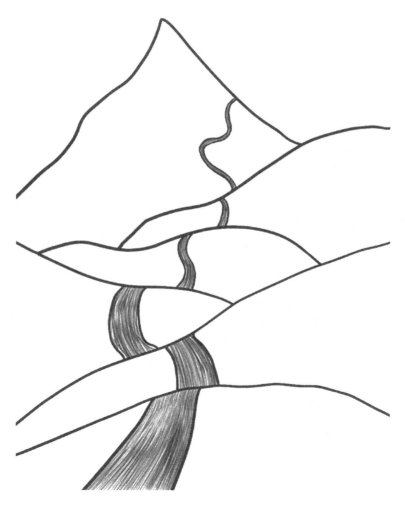

THE GRASS IS GREENER
ON THE OTHER SIDE

I was excited to write this chapter. The illustration I have says it better than I can describe in words. But I will try anyway and then will give you the self-explanatory illustration.

We often think that some other place is better, that being in other people's shoes is easier, that our neighbor has it together, that their lawn is greener than ours, that someone is prettier, and so on. With all those thoughts, we lose appreciation for what we do have in our life. And believe me, many people think the same about you, that you have it together and live in a paradise.

As you know from the beginning of the book, my sister arrived in the US in 2022 as a refugee due to the war in Ukraine. It was a difficult process for her and still isn't easy. She worked jobs she never did in her life, she learned a language she never spoke, and the cultural shock was a lot to handle. She came here with her daughter, and everything has been a struggle, even with a lot of help from me and my husband. She works a lot and only has just enough to make ends meet every month. Life in Ukraine was much easier. Nevertheless, she gets a lot of comments and messages from her so-called friends on social media and in person that she lives an easygoing life and has no problems, not as they are over there.

I understand that people in Ukraine have it very hard right now, but not all refugees have it easy just because they left the country. They fight their own battles and go through difficult times as well.

We like to think that someone else has it better, but what if we started to think that we have it better than someone else? Would it make us appreciate our circumstances a little bit more?

Why It Happens

There are a few reasons why we might think the grass is greener on the other side.

It's common to compare ourselves to others and focus on their successes while feeling down about our own lives. However, this type of thinking can often lead us to believe that others have it better than we do. While comparison can motivate us, it can also make us feel jealous and unhappy.

This type of mindset can cause us to obsess over what we lack, such as a better job, house, or significant other. It's important to remember that the grass isn't always greener on the other side. By taking chances and trying new things, we can break free from this cycle and find happiness in our own lives.

How To Crack This Wall

It's time to break free from the limiting mindset that "the grass is always greener on the other side" when we express dissatisfaction with our own situation. We must appreciate what we have and take actionable steps to improve our lives. Recognizing the value of our current circumstances is crucial, and we must work towards making them better.

You can start by saying something like:

I appreciate what I have and what I can do with it.

Ask yourself these questions:

What can I appreciate today?

What do I have that others don't?

YOU GET WHAT YOU GET, AND YOU DON'T THROW A FIT

I often hear this phrase in daycares and schools, told by teachers to our young children. When teachers use it, I am sure they don't realize the belief they are instilling into children's minds.

This belief builds a giant wall that can translate into many areas of our lives. This wall can feel like we have no say in our life's direction. The sense of powerlessness can be overwhelming and lead to a belief that our paths are predetermined.

If we start to believe that we should not "throw a fit" when we are unhappy, we may bottle up our emotions and feelings. From Part III of this book, we know where that can lead us: not just to mental problems but to health issues as well.

If we believe that we cannot change our circumstances, we are less likely to stand up for ourselves or fight for what we think is right. It can translate into others taking advantage of us as well.

Why It Happens

"We are what we think. All that we are arises with our thoughts. With our thoughts, we make our world."—**Buddha**

It is hard to avoid repeating the same phrases we heard from our parents to our own children. The only way out is to become conscious and aware of your thoughts and destroy your personal walls before you start building the same you had in your children's minds.

Do you remember the internal and external loci of control? If not, here is the meaning again:

"Locus of control is how much individuals perceive that they themselves have control over their own actions as opposed to events in life occurring instead because of external forces. It is measured along a dimension of 'high internal' to 'high external.'"[62]

People with an internal locus of control are happier in their lives and careers. But, like an external locus of control, this wall puts you in the corner of giving all your power to outside circumstances and other people, and it can create a lot of negative feelings and emotions and no motivation to change anything.

How To Crack This Wall

You can start by saying something like:

I am in control of my life, and I can get what I want and express my emotions.

Ask yourself these questions:

Where and how often did I hear this phrase before?

How does it influence my life?

What if I could get anything I wished?

What if it were okay to express my emotions?

---

62 "Locus of Control Theory In Psychology: Internal vs External," November 3, 2022. https://www. simplypsychology.org/locus-of-control.html.

YOU CAN ONLY MAKE MONEY WITH A DEGREE

The more I see students graduating from various schools and not getting the career they studied for, the more it proves that a degree does not always mean a well-paid job, and sometimes you can make more money without a degree than with one.

Here is a story from my classmates that I remember, and you might have a similar one too. Most of my high school classmates in Ukraine went on to college or university to study. But a few who weren't good in school didn't continue their studies. Well, those few had already been making money for five years by the time we graduated college, and some had even established their small businesses.

I see the same thing in the US: people who get a degree sometimes can't find a job in their desired career for years, and some end up in low-paying jobs just so they can support themselves *and* pay back their student loans. Others with simple certifications are further along on their journey to making money.

After moving here, a few of my friends decided to continue their studies. I was considering it too because I felt that my two degrees from Ukraine and Poland didn't mean anything in the US. I would have to prove myself all over again to be able to gain a high-paying job. Well, I held back, hoping I could find a way up without undergoing another four years of education just to prove that I could do what I was already doing well.

But I knew several immigrants who studied anywhere from two to eight years so they could be someone in this country. Of course, student loans were involved because there was no way they could pay for their studies with a low hourly rate. They graduated and spent years looking for a job. Many of them didn't find one and gave up on the idea, returning to what they were doing before. Others did get a job only to see that the pay was not much greater but almost the same, but now with the added problem of having loans of $25K to $100K to pay back.

Of course, it is not every story out there. I am just trying to say that holding a degree doesn't mean making a lot of money, and no degree doesn't mean you can't make a lot of money.

There is always a way to make money with minimum official education and maximum investment in yourself through self-education.

You can be a self-taught artist, musician, salesperson, businessperson, and so much more, and make plenty of money. I agree that some professions require a degree, so if you want to be a doctor or a lawyer, you need to study for it; there is no way around it, at least in this country.

Why It Happens

In the past, only people with status and money could access higher education, so they took high-paying jobs and continued their generational wealth. People of the land simply could not afford it or didn't want to lose their working hands on the farm or wherever they were needed. So we kept believing that only the privileged could get a degree, and only they could make good money. This is how we developed a stigma that says, Degree = Money, and No Degree = No Money.

But in our fast-changing world, it doesn't play out like this anymore. There are many rich and famous people who didn't get their degree, and no one cares. Bill Gates is a Harvard dropout. Michael Dell was a freshman at the University of Texas at Austin when he decided to drop out. Richard Branson dropped out of school due to struggles with dyslexia and poor academic performance. Larry Ellison dropped out of college twice and was told by his adoptive father that he would never amount to anything. You might not know some of these names, but all of them are billionaires. And they did it without an official degree.

How To Crack This Wall

When I came here, I kept telling myself that I didn't need an official paper to prove that I was worth making as much money as I needed, whether $50K, $100K, or more.

You can start by saying something like:

A degree doesn't mean making a lot of money, and no degree doesn't mean I can't make a lot of money.

Ask yourself these questions:

What if I could make more money without a degree than with one?

What could be the big idea on how to do it?

What do other people without a degree do to make money?

THE APPLE DOESN'T FALL FAR FROM THE TREE

I totally get it when people say that kids inherit traits from their parents, both good and bad. But here's the thing: every person, parent or child, is totally unique and has the power to create their own destiny.

I would not want to be compared to my dad. He had several negative characteristics, like alcoholism and selfishness. Those are two things I avoid in my life because I saw how destructive they were.

Another thing I hate is when parents compare their children to each other, saying, "You are just like your mother," (or like your father) in a negative way. There are many examples to the contrary, of children of broken parents becoming amazing people who put themselves into the world only in a positive way.

If you were told all your childhood that you were just like your mother or just like your father, and you only saw what could be wrong with you because of that, it is time to break your internal wall and remember that you are unique, that you have the power to write your destiny, and to do what is right for you.

I will share with you something really personal: I got my DNA tested several years ago. What I found there wasn't good news. I read the report of faults from all my family members. I got them all… just to list a few: alcohol and nicotine addictions, gambling, obesity, high blood cholesterol… After reading it, I felt like I had inherited all the negative traits that exist.

But I have never believed that. I had two choices: to accept what my DNA told me about myself, or look nature in the face and say, "I decide who I will be, and it is only in my hands not to trigger the negative attributes."

Why It Happens

We inherit a lot from our parents: looks, habits, how we speak, and sometimes more. If some things we can't change… well, nowadays, everything is possible… for others, we are totally responsible, and it is only our decision what we will become. While we grow up with other people's opinions, it is our choice to believe them or not.

How To Crack This Wall

You can start by saying something like:

I am in control of my own destiny.

Ask yourself these questions:

What traits would I like to inherit?

What would I like to leave behind?

What would I like to change?

MONEY CAN'T BUY HAPPINESS

Money or happiness? Most people have an answer in the first few seconds: 99% want happiness.

Can money buy happiness? YES or NO?

"Money can't buy happiness. But neither can poverty."—**Leo Rosten**

At some point in my life, I thought, *NO, money can't buy happiness.* You know why I thought that (I didn't have enough)!

But apparently, YES, it can, according to the University of Pennsylvania:

"The National Academy of Science, in its research in 2021, tested more than 33,000 people to see how their annual income was proportional to their life satisfaction and well-being.

"The results were incredible; for up to $75,000 for a household, people said they lived a much less satisfying life. At $75K, you start to feel stable, I would say, and going beyond $75K, your life satisfaction and well-being keep on climbing."[63]

So, might we say that happiness is connected to how much money we make? Absolutely.

Let's revisit Abraham Maslow's Hierarchy of Needs. We can't satisfy our basic needs without making a certain amount of money in our modern world. To cover food, water, and shelter, we need to pay our bills. In the survival stage, we experience different feelings like fear, anxiety, and other negative emotions that make it impossible for us to be happy before meeting our basic needs.[64]

---

63 Penn Today. "Money Matters to Happiness—Perhaps More than Previously Thought," January 18, 2021. https://penntoday.upenn.edu/news/money-matters-to-happiness-perhaps-more-than-previously-thought.
64 *Maslow's Hierarchy of Needs.* 3 Nov. 2022, https://www.simplypsychology.org/maslow.html.

The more money we make, the closer we get to the top of the pyramid, where we can try to reach our self-fulfillment needs by creating, giving, exploring, and looking for our purpose.

Why It Happens

Just like a lot of other phrases, this was repeated to me a lot throughout my young life. It made me believe that financial stability doesn't mean anything and that you can be happy without money. Of course, you can't buy important things in life like love, care, kindness, relationships, understanding, and much more. But nevertheless, in our modern world, money plays a big role in how happy we are.

Did you know that one of the top five reasons for divorce is financial instability?

How To Crack This Wall

Ask yourself these questions:

How much money do I need to feel financially secure and cover the first two levels of the pyramid?

What if I made less money? How would that make me feel?

What if I could make all the money I need? What would I do then?

YOUR PAST DETERMINES YOUR FUTURE

There is no doubt that your past has influenced who you are today.

"When the pain overtakes you, reach inside. Gather the broken pieces, and hand them to God. Ask Him to remake your heart. Different, this time. Stronger. More beautiful. This is how we are made, and remade by the Maker."
—**Yasmin Mogahed**

Even though your past has influenced who you are today, it doesn't decide who you can be tomorrow because today is the day when everything can change, and all your broken pieces of this wall can come together in a magic way to pave the road to your future.

This wall can hold you back by making you believe that you only have what you had in the past, and it will play on a loop over and over again. It can blind you from the lessons you were supposed to learn through experience, and it will lock your potential behind prison bars.

Why It Happens

I believe that we will encounter the same challenges until we learn what God or the Universe is trying to teach us in this life. But if you don't get the lesson, if you don't realize it and learn from it, you will continue to find yourself in the same shitty situations over and over again.

So stop and ask yourself, all the time, *What lessons was I taught?* Can you stop the Universe from throwing at you the same pile of shit by finally realizing some inevitable truths like this one, that your past doesn't determine your future?

How To Crack This Wall

If you find yourself standing behind this self-built wall, you can start taking some bricks off it right now by:

Reframing your past experiences. Look at all those horrible, difficult, or failed moments and ask yourself what good you got from them. What did you learn? How did your experiences make you stronger?

Focusing on now. Today is the day that can change everything. The past is over, and the future is not yet here. The only thing you have control over is you, right now, at this moment. So ask yourself, what future do you desire? How do you want tomorrow to be different from today? How will the decision you are making right now influence your tomorrow?

Visualizing. Imagine what your life could be like in a year or in five years. Picture your desired outcome and think about what needs to happen from today till that picture in your head to make it all true.

You can start by saying something like:

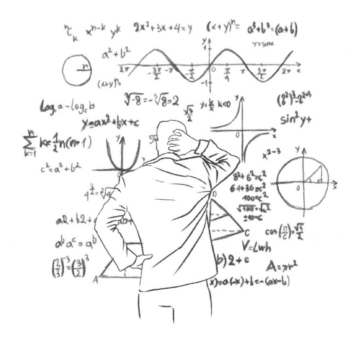

I learned many lessons, and today I can decide what my future holds.

THIS IS TRADITION

Traditions are important. They keep our culture alive and remind us where we came from. There are many good traditions that we want to remember and continue to pass on from generation to generation, but there are also many traditions that are ridiculous, and that go against human rights and our inner feeling of what is just for us and for others.

Do you think horrible and harmful traditions don't exist in our modern world? Think again.

There are traditions that were practiced hundreds of years ago that are still alive today. Some of them are horrible and should finally become echoes of the past. They only live on because parents teach them to their children.

I found a few examples I wanted to share with you, just to illustrate that not all traditions are good and should be blindly followed. My first realization of such traditions came in 2009 when I watched the movie *Desert Flower*. The film is based on the life of Waris Dirie, an international supermodel who began life as a member of a nomadic tribe in Somalia where female genital mutilation is still practiced. To this day, even though it is officially banned in those countries, the tradition is still alive. If you like to watch documentaries about far-off countries, you probably know that there are many others similar to this one.

The passion gap, or Cape Flats smile, is another interesting tradition. This dental trend originated in Cape Flats, Cape Town, South Africa, involving the intentional removal of upper front teeth for fashion and status.

In the same vein are traditions for finger amputation, lip plating, tongue severing, neck rings, breast ironing, and marrying girls as young as 11 years old. And if you think such traditions only exist in third-world countries, you are mistaken: "in Colorado, more than 5,000 minors have been married since the year 2000. In most states, the minimum age for marriage is 18, but many, including Colorado, allow for exceptions."[65]

So while some traditions are good, others require some deep rethinking of why they are still alive. If your mind wall tells you this is tradition and you must follow it, but for wherever reason, it feels wrong in your heart or your gut, you are probably right.

Why It Happens

Traditions, just like many beliefs, are passed from generation to generation without questioning if they serve us anymore. They are usually taught to us from a young age, making us believe that they are dictating what is the right and the only way.

How To Crack This Wall

Breaking the belief of an unwanted tradition can be difficult, but it is possible.

Do your research. Learn about this tradition. Where did it come from? Why was it created? Are there any health concerns about it?

Talk to others. Connect with individuals who hold similar beliefs about the tradition. They can offer you support and help you discover valuable resources to aid you on your path.

Challenge the tradition. Take a moment to reflect on your beliefs surrounding the tradition and assess if there are valid reasons to continue holding on to them.

Take steps. Declining to participate in some part of the tradition could be a good beginning for you.

Be patient. Breaking the belief of an unwanted tradition takes a lot of time and effort. And if you can avoid or decline this tradition, it might continue for others. Deciding if you want to do something about it or escape your fate is good enough.

---

65 Dukakis, Andrea. "Child Marriage, Common In The Past, Persists Today." Colorado Public Radio. Accessed July 31, 2023. https://www.cpr.org/show-segment/child-marriage-common-in-the-past-persists-today/.

You can start by saying something like:

Not all traditions must be followed.

Ask yourself this question:

What makes me feel that this tradition is holding me back?

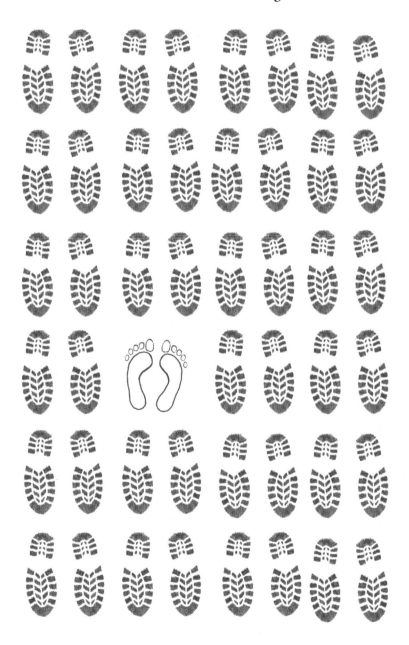

LIFE IS A COMPETITION

"The world has enough for everyone's need, but not enough for everyone's greed." **Mahatma Gandhi**

We used to believe that surviving is for the strongest and that life is a competition. But many studies have proven that people thrive and succeed in society when we cooperate instead of when we compete.

In the article "Why to cooperate is better than to compete," the National Institutes of Health conclude that:

"If you're outgoing and like to collaborate, you're more likely to think highly of yourself when it comes to work and social status. Researchers found that people with higher levels of what they call behavioral approach system (BAS) tend to have better cognitive abilities and feel like they're higher up on the social ladder."[66]

Working together with others can actually boost our mental well-being. Because when we see life as a constant competition, it can be overwhelming to always compare ourselves to others and feel like we're not measuring up. This causes anxiety and stress, making it tough to enjoy life and be productive. Instead, focusing on cooperation can help us feel more fulfilled and less weighed down by stress. Conversely, when we are focused only on winning, we might overstep our personal values or forget to live in the moment.

If there is enough for everyone in this world, competition will get you somewhere, but cooperation will get you even farther.

---

66 Balconi, Michela, Davide Crivelli, and Maria Elide Vanutelli. "Why to Cooperate Is Better than to Compete: Brain and Personality Components." *BMC Neuroscience* 18 (September 20, 2017): 68. https://doi.org/10.1186/s12868-017-0386-8.

Why It Happens

Growing up, we were taught that we must constantly compete with others to gain our parents' attention, secure our place in the world, and earn everything that comes our way. But what if we realized that these things are already available to us? How much lighter would our burdens be, and how much more joyous would our lives become if we simply embraced what we have and focused on giving and receiving love?

How To Crack This Wall

You can start by saying something like:

Life is cooperation.

Take a moment to observe your surroundings in nature. Do you notice any signs of competition or cooperation? I believe that if nature were constantly competing, there wouldn't be much greenery or life to speak of. Instead, it's through the harmonious collaboration of all living things that something truly beautiful is created.

Ask yourself these questions:

What makes me want to compete?

What if I believed that there is enough for everyone?

What can change if I cooperate?

A BIRD IN THE HAND IS
WORTH TWO IN THE BUSH

What bird are you holding? Do you even like it? Is it pretty, and can it sing? Or are you just holding a goose that pinched all your hands? Nothing against geese here, but holding onto something doesn't mean it is good.

I took Dave Ramsey's Financial Peace University years ago with my husband, and by the way, it helped us tremendously. In the last class, I heard this: if you clench your hands to hold on tight to something, there is no way for you to receive anymore because your hands are already preoccupied with what you already have. But if you open your hands in a giving way and just keep them open, what is yours will stay, and what is not will go, but other things that were meant to be for you will come. I don't know if they said it in those exact words, but this is how I understood it and remembered it for more than eight years now.

So holding on to that one bird that might not even be yours is a little bit selfish too. In my previous book, I had a great example regarding this matter for your career. Imagine that about 50% of people hate their jobs, which means they're in the wrong place and possibly taking someone else's spot who might love to do what they are doing. Don't for a second think it is impossible. If there are undertakers, coroners, and forensic pathologists who love what they do, then there is someone to love your clerk or accounting job that you hate. Why don't you leave it for them and find a place where you feel happier and more passionate?

This applies not just to our careers but to other aspects of our life:

Career: A person who is afraid to leave their secure job may never pursue their passion. And in the meantime, they are occupying someone else's dream job.

Relationships: A person staying in a toxic relationship will never find their true love.

Finance: A person afraid to invest their money may never grow their wealth.

Travel: A person who is afraid to travel to new countries may never experience the richness of different cultures and open their mind to something different.

Why It Happens

Once again, this is an echo of the past, when we were told to be content with what we have and not risk anything because of the possibility of something going wrong… but that's just fear talking.

Change is part of life; if there is no change, there is no life.

How To Crack This Wall

Think about the potential benefit of taking the risk. What could you gain by letting that one bird out of your hands?

You can start by saying something like:

I can gain more by letting go.

Ask yourself these questions:

What makes me think I need to hold on to what I have?

What is there for me if I let go?

How can letting go be beneficial to myself and others?

ALL GREAT THINGS WERE
ALREADY INVENTED

When I started my first CAM (Community Association Management) job, I was told by an older gentleman not to reinvent the wheel, and that everything worked the way it was meant to. I just needed to get in and continue the spin of the old squeaky wheel. Nevertheless, when I realized how rotted the wheel was and how much noise was made while spinning, I reinvented every part of it and set it on autopilot.

I started with one little thing, and about nine months later, when I got everything functioning, every single system was reinvented or adjusted. Even the old maintenance schedule that seemed to work... really didn't. It was not productive and a waste of HOA money.

We often think the wheel is working, even if it is rusted, squeaky, and absorbs 10 times more oil. Until we really reinvent it and see how much better it could be, maybe a new wheel wasn't needed but a conveyer belt instead.

A lot of things were invented. You are absolutely right on this one. Some blow your mind, making you wonder how it is possible, and some come under a big question: WHY? Why do we even need this? But people don't stop with what they have; they keep inventing and reinventing things. And just by putting some things together, you can make something absolutely new and stunning that no one thought of before.

You know, I heard that all great things were already written and said... but they weren't written or said by me, and I can shine a light on something from my unique perspective (or maybe even not that unique)... but if it catches someone's attention, and helps them to see it better, I did my job.

But if I believed that first sentence, I would never have sat down to write my first book, and this book would never have come to be either. But nevertheless, it was born, and you are holding it right now. It might not be the best book you have ever read, but it has the right to exist because someone once again decided to reinvent the wheel.

Why It Happens

We say that to ourselves out of fear of failing or of not being recognized for our work. We say, "Why try if someone already did it?" But that someone wasn't you, and you might hold the key to that brand new invention the world was desperately hoping for.

How To Crack This Wall

Be open to seeing the same things from a new angle, and you might surprise yourself one day.

You can start by saying something like:

Even if it was invented, it wasn't invented by me.

Ask yourself these questions:

What idea am I holding back?

What makes me think that what I have to offer is not valuable?

What can make it valuable?

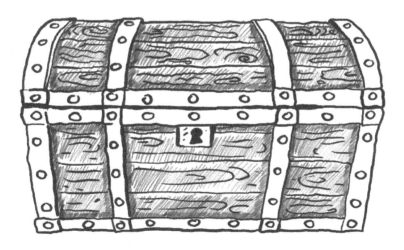

YOU CAN'T HAVE YOUR CAKE AND EAT IT TOO

Have you heard this from your parents? They probably told you that you could only have one good thing at a time, like, "Don't hope to have two toys that you like at the same time." Getting older, it changed to "You can't be in two places at once" or "If you are at work, you can't also be at home with your family."

Now we all know after Covid happened, everything changed. You can work from home, or make your work *work* for you while you are enjoying your family. Some people still believe that you can't have a successful career and a perfect home life, that there will always be some trade-offs... and I say, decide what your priority is and set good boundaries.

The belief that we must give up something in order to achieve something else can hinder us from taking risks and achieving our goals. For instance, if we aspire to start a business but feel we must surrender our current job and social life, we might not take the necessary steps to make it happen. Well, if you know how a lot of other people started their businesses, including me, most do it by building detour roads. I talked about this metaphor in my first book, *I Know What You Need To Succeed*.

This belief can also make us feel like we are constantly losing and preventing progress because it doesn't matter what we do, it is never good enough and doesn't pay off to gain several things we want. Furthermore, this belief can result in negative self-talk, leading us to doubt our abilities and potential for success.

Why It Happens

It's understandable why this proverb resonates with so many people. It's a simple concept that makes sense—once you eat the cake, it's gone, and you can't have it again. Or can you?

We all know from experience that we can't have everything we want. For example, if we indulge in cake, we might not be able to achieve our desired weight. Similarly, if we want to be rich, we might have to sacrifice our free time or family time. It has been around long enough and made us believe that we have to make compromises.

Ultimately, this proverb reminds us to be realistic with our expectations.

How To Crack This Wall

Just like with that bird in the hand... we think if we have one, we can't have the other. A lot of these proverbs tell us similar things. They limit us in one way or the other. But none of this is a rule, and a lot of them don't work anymore and don't serve us in our life.

You can start by saying something like:

I am not limited to one good thing. There are more good things for me.

Ask yourself these questions:

What makes me feel that way?

How can I get more *and* not lose out?

Why is it not true for me?

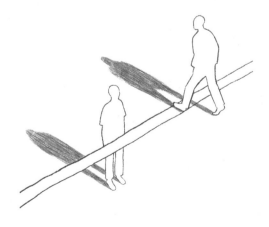

PICK THE LOWEST-
HANGING FRUIT FIRST

So often, we start with the easiest thing on our schedules and to-do lists, or when we set out on the path to achieving our goals, this is known as "picking the lowest-hanging fruit." While it might be tempting, this is often not the best option. The opposite might in fact be your absolute best solution or approach in many situations:

"Some productivity experts believe that by starting on your quickest, simplest tasks first, you build momentum that carries you through to the harder tasks. However, other experts believe that completing your hardest tasks first is the key to getting things done more efficiently. Research shows that people who execute their most difficult tasks first are generally more productive and high achieving than those who start easy and work their way up."[67]

I see this often with my clients. Their to-do lists are overwhelmed with things that are not that important or that could be done but by someone else. Hustling through small things, they never get to the big, important stuff. And that happens day in and day out... at the end of the year, they realize they never got to the essential things, so they never reached their goal. Has it happened to you?

Here is my example of when I decided to write this book. I finally left my CAM job and started to work from home on my own business. I was so happy that I finally had more time to do what was important to me... well, I really hoped that would be the case.

But for some reason, I ended up with less time for important business tasks and more time for other things, like housework. My husband was now expecting me to do more around the house and take care of our

---

67 "Hardest or Easiest Work First? What the Research Shows - The Productive Engineer," September 18, 2019. https://theproductiveengineer.net/hardest-or-easiest-work-first-what-the-research-shows/.

child. Every single day started with picking up toys, vacuuming, doing dishes, and cleaning.

I honestly was surprised… where did all this come from? I didn't have that much when I worked full-time at one job, part-time at my business, and still was running the household. But the weirdest thing was that when I got my house chores done, cooked, worked out, and picked up my niece from school, I only had one hour left before running to daycare to get my child. And that was on a day when I didn't have any coaching calls.

Sometimes that hour was enough to finish one chapter of my book, and sometimes sitting in front of the computer gathering my thoughts together would put me close to the end of that one hour. And with 15 minutes left in my time bank for the day, I thought, *What is the point of starting? Fifteen minutes would not be enough anyway, and tomorrow it won't be easy to pick up where I left off.*

This happened for a few weeks until I realized it wasn't working… my book wasn't moving forward as fast as I had anticipated. I thought something had to change, and I needed to *start* with what was important to me instead. So I turned my day around and began by writing the book, and for the last hour before I would pick up my child, I cleaned as much as possible. Just that one simple switch gave me an additional hour of book writing and researching in the morning. And I was still able to do everything else. But most importantly, I started to see progress in my book. Chapters got written faster, and I felt I was on track to finish it by midsummer 2023.

Why It Happens

If your brain says, *Let's do the easy tasks first*, you're not alone. Recent research by Maryam Kouchaki suggests that people gravitate toward simpler tasks when struggling with a heavy workload. However, they find that the strategy doesn't pay off in the long run. "When we are overwhelmed and busy, we just go with easier tasks, and the difficult tasks tend to pile up," Kouchaki says.[68]

---

68 Kellogg Insight. "Why You Should Skip the Easy Wins and Tackle the Hard Task First," November 4, 2019. https://insight.kellogg.northwestern.edu/article/easy-or-hard-tasks-first.

And it is not just that our brains are naturally geared towards seeking short-term rewards, which can lead us toward actions that provide immediate gratification. As a result, we tend to favor familiar paths that require minimal effort.

How To Crack This Wall

Stop what you are doing right now and ask yourself:

What is the most important thing for me today?

Is what I am doing now important or distracting from what is important?

What if I put the most important thing at the top of my list and did it first?

What tasks am I afraid of doing?

What is stopping me from setting priorities?

How can I change my schedule to do what is important first thing in the morning?

OUT OF SIGHT, OUT OF MIND

"I forgave him and let go, but absolutely can't see him or anything that relates to him." My friend told me that several years after her divorce. She explained to me that the saying "Out of sight, out of mind" applies to her situation.

I listened attentively and asked her these thought-provoking questions: "What makes you think you really forgave him and let go? What is so difficult about seeing him or anything related to him?" She looked confused and said, "I was absolutely sure that I let him go, I thought. But every time I see something, it triggers all the memories and negative feelings. I just don't need to see him."

However, I realized that even though we may think we have moved on, the negative emotions and effects may still be present in our system and body. We might think, *As long as I don't see it and don't think about it, I am safe…* but are we really? Did we really heal and let it go? Well, if an image triggers a flood of negative emotions and thoughts, we probably did not heal as much as we thought. Avoiding an image is not a complete solution, as it may still weigh us down like a heavy backpack.

You might think, *How is this a wall? How is this limiting me?* First, we all know that not seeing something doesn't mean we won't think about it repeatedly and relive our past. Second, if an image triggers everything back, deep healing is needed.

If you continue to believe this nonsense, you might never heal completely. You might push away the real problem by hiding or closing your eyes and turning away, hoping it will disappear on its own magically resolve itself.

Why It Happens

It is great to be optimistic, but sometimes we need a reality check. Closing your eyes or turning away won't work forever; at one point, you will need to realize and accept the problem, and after putting your adult pants on, find a solution or know what steps need to be taken.

I talked with my friend today about how some people are not just optimistic but blindly optimistic. It happens more often than you think, sometimes with big things like illnesses and sometimes with small things like plastic bottles on the beach. We choose to turn away and not act because dealing with it requires more work and some serious commitment.

How To Crack This Wall

Choose to solve the problem instead of just turning away from it.

You can start by saying something like:

I can choose to face the situation and find a solution.

Ask yourself these questions:

Where am I closing my eyes, hoping that I don't have to deal with it if I don't see it?

What if I finally faced it head-on and do what needs to be done?

What can I unload from my backpack by simply dealing with it?

IT IS NOT MEANT TO BE

"Never let life impede on your ability to manifest your dreams. Dig deeper into your dreams and deeper into yourself and believe that anything is possible, and make it happen."—**Corin Nemec**

Oh, how often I hear people give up way too soon... calming themselves down with the phrase, "It is just not meant to be" or "It is just not meant to happen for me." Even in my family, I heard way too often, "It is what it is," meaning I came here with my past, but I don't think I can do anything now to change my future.

Sometimes, we use these sayings to face our past and keep moving forward. Yet, it can also be a way to reassure ourselves of our less-than-ideal circumstances and fate. If we firmly believe that it is not meant to be, we will not find a way to do something to change it. We will put our hands down and continue on the same path, believing that a certain outcome is already written for us.

We build this wall with the help of others who may have failed once or twice but didn't try long enough to succeed. And maybe you have been swayed by the negativity of those around you who doubt their capabilities and, as a result, yours when it comes to achieving goals or doing something extraordinary.

We don't try to analyze the situation or change different variables. If we try changing one thing 50 times in a row and it still doesn't work, maybe it needs to be changed differently, or another component needs to be looked at instead. In the end, there are many variables that can be changed to achieve what you want. If one thing doesn't work, try adjusting the other. For example, don't give up if changing your diet didn't help you get to your dream weight; exercise, and work on your mindset. It could be your mindset holding your extra 10 pounds on because you just believe it is not meant to be, or your parents always told you that you are on the bigger side, and you can't seem to shake that off.

Why It Happens

We build this wall for many reasons. Here are a few:

Maybe you've had setbacks or disappointments in the past, which can make it seem like success is impossible.

Other people may have told you that your goals are too hard to reach.

You might not take risks or try new things when you're afraid to fail.

If you don't feel good about yourself, you might think you're incapable of achieving what you want. This can lead to a self-fulfilling prophecy, where you start to act in a way to fulfill your own (false) beliefs. So then you announce, "I told you. It is not meant to be for me."

Sometimes, you might have a fixed mindset, believing you can't change or improve.

How To Crack This Wall

You can start by saying something like:

The past is past, the future is uncertain, and I can act now to change the impossible.

Ask yourself these questions:

What if it is meant to be if I only changed one thing?

What would it be?

How can I prove to myself that it is meant to be?

What do I need to do to break this wall?

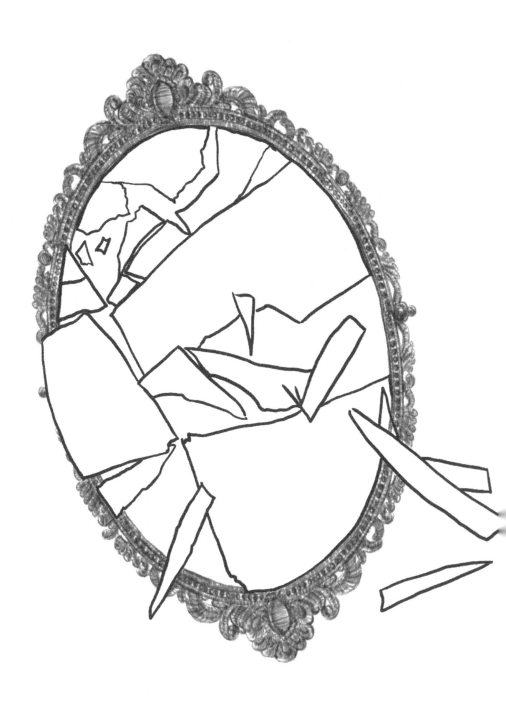

ASKING FOR HELP IS A SIGN OF WEAKNESS

*"Therefore I tell you, whatever you ask in prayer, believe that you have received it, and it will be yours."—**Mark 11:24***

The Bible talks a lot about asking for help, especially when you are in need. I believe the Bible is another manifestation guide; if you read it right, you can get many universal secrets from it.

But I was one of those who thought for a long time—for about 30 years, in fact—that asking for help is showing your weakness, telling others that you are not capable of managing your own life, accepting defeat, and all manner of disparaging thoughts.

My mom did a good job raising me to be independent and, yes, in a package with that came: don't ask for help, don't complain, don't show weakness to others, just walk it off, and so on. Understand I am not blaming her here. I am just glad I realized why I had this wall and why it was so difficult to tell someone I needed help. Otherwise, I would have continued to go through rough times alone.

So why are we so afraid to be vulnerable for a minute and ask for help or tell someone we need support? Brené Brown says that showing your vulnerability is the greatest measure of courage:

*"Vulnerability is not winning or losing; it's having the courage to show up and be seen when we have no control over the outcome. Vulnerability is not weakness; it's our greatest measure of courage."—**Brené Brown***

Why It Happens

We all have our own reasons why we are afraid to ask for help. Here are a few common ones:

You may have been taught, just like me, that it is important to be self-reliant and independent.

You may have been told that asking for help is a sign of failure. "Figure it out on your own!" people told you every time you came to ask something.

You may think you will be judged or rejected if you ask for help.

You don't want to bother others. They probably have a lot on their plate already.

You're too proud when it comes to asking for help. You are afraid of losing face, your status, or your social media avatar of an always happy person.

You may not know how to ask for help. You simply don't know how to approach someone and what to say. Sometimes three simple words are enough: "I need help."

How To Crack This Wall

Think of the benefits of asking for help. Start with small things if you don't feel comfortable asking for a big favor. Remember, everyone needs help once in a while, and it is okay to be vulnerable.

You can start by saying something like:

I can accept help and ask for help. It will not change who I am.

Ask yourself these questions:

What do I need help with?

How would my life be easier if I asked for help?

What could change if I accepted other people's help?

I had a problem with that last one too. I could not accept help even when others were offering it. You can read more about it in my first book, *I Know What You Need To Succeed.*

TO GIVE MORE, WE NEED TO RECEIVE MORE FIRST

"In everything I have shown you that, by working hard, we must
help the weak. In this way we remember the Lord Jesus' words:
'It is more blessed to give than to receive.'"—Acts 20:35

Many young people, and some not-so-young people, think, *I will*
love you more if you do this or that; I will donate if I make more money; I
will work out if I get more free time; I will be happy when I have this dream
job, car, or house. We all sometimes think, *If I could only get this, then I will*
be… or I will do…

But did you know that the idea of needing to receive more in order to
give more is just a myth? In fact, the truth is quite the opposite. Giving can
actually lead to receiving even more in return. This is because giving is like
a form of energy that attracts even more energy back to us.

I know there is one universal law about this: never expect a return
from the same place you gave to. It doesn't matter if it was love, energy,
money, effort, or anything else. If you give, just give because you wish to do
so without expecting anything in return. And don't worry if it doesn't come
back from the same place. It will come back from somewhere else.

I know many people who get frustrated and upset after helping someone and then asking for something in return (or not even asking but believing that person now owes them) only to be rejected or misunderstood.

Most people have heard of karma, the idea that the energy you give
off will return to you somehow. To receive more, you need to give more
which is a universal truth, but don't forget to love yourself at the same
time. Give with an open heart and open hands. Don't expect to receive; just

continue living your life, and the energy will come back to you, maybe in another form and from an absolutely unexpected source.

One more important note here: if you are giving in the hope of receiving something back, like a trade, talk about this with the person upfront so there are no unfulfilled expectations, and so that a grudge won't grow in you if you don't receive anything in return. We may end up feeling resentful if we don't get what we think we deserve. This can cause negative feelings like anger, bitterness, and envy, which we already know can negatively impact our mental and physical health. If you didn't read the feelings and emotions part of the book, look up at least a few of those I just mentioned.

Why It Happens

Many of us are taught to believe that life is a series of transactions, especially since money was created—and even before that, if you produced milk but wanted to get bread, you would exchange what you had for what you needed. It can feel like everything comes with a cost, so we want to receive first in order to give and share what we have. We are afraid to come up empty-handed. We believe there is not enough to go around, so we must hoard our resources. We may be afraid that we will not have enough for ourselves if we give too much. But remember, in one of the chapters I shared with you, the concept of open hands: you cannot receive something if your hands are full or if you are holding on to something too tight.

How To Crack This Wall

Start by giving without any expectations. You can begin by offering small gifts like your time, attention, or words of encouragement. Take a moment to appreciate all the wonderful things you already have in your life.

It's an amazing feeling to give without expectation of return, and it comes from a place of love and compassion. This is the most meaningful form of giving and will make you feel happy.

You can start by saying something like:

I receive what I give.

Ask yourself these questions:

What can I give without any expectation for return?

What type of giving will make me fill happy or fulfilled?

What do I want more of?

What could I give in order to receive what I want later?

YOU HAVE TO BE BORN IN A RICH FAMILY TO BE SUCCESSFUL

I already mentioned Dave Ramsey in this book, but I will say a few words about him again because he is a financial guru and taught me a lot about handling money in the US. I am glad I had a chance to read his book early in my immigration journey. Did you know that most millionaires (79%) didn't inherit their wealth from their families? It's true! Instead, they worked hard and made smart financial decisions, according to Dave Ramsey. *The Millionaire Next Door* is another book that supports this theory.

After considering it, being born into a wealthy family might not necessarily lead to success. In fact, it could even have the opposite effect. When children don't appreciate or know how wealth was earned, they flush it down the toilet every chance they have, not thinking about where the money comes from.

Almost all of the great people I know through reading their books and the local people I've interviewed became successful because they weren't born into it. After experiencing suffering and distress, they viewed achieving success and becoming wealthy as their main solution and the only option to escape poverty.

Success is primarily determined not by the money we are given at birth but by the choices we make as individuals. Even if someone is given every advantage, they can still fail if they make poor decisions. Conversely, someone who has worked hard can succeed if they make good choices and don't give up.

You might argue that more money affords you more options and opportunities, and it's true that money helps us with some things. It helped me to self-publish my first book, for example. It is no secret that self-publishing is a major investment, and it would have been easier if I had already had the money required without having to save up and invest over several months to make it all happen. But at the same time, it is part of my success story; I worked for it to become my reality. How much more successful would you feel if everything were given to you without any effort? Let's just say that winning the lottery could fix that problem, right? Well… as surprising as it sounds, research indicates that "70% of lottery winners ultimately find themselves without money, and one in three ends up filing for bankruptcy," as the National Endowment for Financial Education reports.[69]

Of course, there are many other studies that say that being born to a financially stable family gives you better chances to succeed in life, meaning to finish school and college and get a well-paid job. But I think it is all about what you believe and what success means to you.

Why It Happens

Throughout our lives, we have been taught that success is only attainable through the acquisition of wealth. This is a widely held belief in many cultures, including the country I came from, and it is further reinforced by social media and personal experiences. We may observe that those who are born into wealthy families have access to better education, healthcare, and more opportunities, leading us to believe that money is a crucial component to achieving success.

There are many examples of both sides of the coin, people born rich who succeed and those born poor who do it very well, and they have a better story to tell to inspire others. It seems like we all have an equal shot in life, so the main component is not money but YOU.

How To Crack This Wall

Think of five of your favorite successful people. Now equip yourself with Google and find out: Where did they start? Were they born into wealth or not? I am sure you would find that the majority are from regular families like yours and mine.

69 "Research Statistic on Financial Windfalls and Bankruptcy." Accessed July 31, 2023. https://www.nefe.org/news/2018/01/research-statistic-on-financial-windfalls-and-bankruptcy.aspx.

You can start by saying something like:

The main component in being successful is ME.

Ask yourself these questions:

How can I prove to myself that this wall is not true?

What will make me believe that anyone, including myself, can be successful?

SUCCESS IS ABOUT WHAT OTHER PEOPLE SEE AND THINK OF ME

We are all hooked on what other people think of us. We want to fit in, to feel part of a group, and that often means caring about what the group members think of us.

After publishing my first book, I got some interesting comments from those who didn't read the book but read the title. They looked at me, an immigrant woman in her early thirties, and asked what I had done so that I could teach them how to be successful too. They said things like, "I didn't see you on a magazine cover or hear about you on TV. Did you make a million dollars by chance?" And they were right: none of that had happened for me YET.

But if they had read my story, they would know my success wasn't determined by a million dollars at that stage of my life. Instead my success was determined by where I had started and how far I had come, going through all the obstacles life threw at me. It was about how, at an early age, I could challenge myself to live a better life than my parents and to take risks that were sometimes dangerous.

But for those who decided to take a couple of hours and read the book, there were no questions, and the reviews speak for themselves. People much older and wiser than me found the piece of advice or inspiration they had been looking for for years.

So remember this one thing about success: the idea of success is unique to each person, so what you consider success may not be and shouldn't be the same as what I consider it. For me, it is a success to be where I am in life and to be able to write my second book. For you, success might be absolutely different. It could be not having panic attacks daily, being able to eat healthy foods, taking your child to school every day, just getting out of bed in the morning, or maybe making those million dollars, for God's sake. But it is definitely not if other people consider you successful because I will tell you for sure, for many people, I might not be considered successful because their understanding of success is different than mine.

One more thing: don't be fooled by pictures of celebrities and other people you follow on social media, thinking they have it together; their life is perfect; they made it. Everyone has struggles and imperfections that are usually not shared with the public to support that brand or face.

Once, I was contacted by a man on Instagram who looked rich and happy by his profile. I thought, *What could I possibly do for this "has it all" guy?* He scheduled a consultation with me, and at the consultation, I found out he was about to file for bankruptcy and was suffering a lot with his money habits and decision-making. Who would have known? That is definitely not what his profile says. On the other hand, I know some wealthy folks who dress in Walmart and never show off their wealth. They love their simple life and don't care what other people see or think.

Why It Happens

It's common for many people to worry about not being liked or accepted by others. This can cause them to focus a lot on what others think of them and try hard to show a perfect picture to the world just to avoid rejection. This fear may come from a lack of self-confidence, where they don't value themselves highly enough and look for validation from others, believing that their success depends on others' approval. But often, chasing others' perspectives of success makes us extremely miserable because it is not what we wanted in the first place. We could wish to simply be able to return to our family for dinner instead of working 24/7 to make someone believe that we made it in life.

How To Crack This Wall

Identify what success means for you. Think of it in detail. If it concerns your career, try to think of what would make you proud of yourself.

You can start by saying something like:

My success is determined by me only.

Ask yourself these questions:

What will make me proud of myself?

What must happen for me to think I am successful?

What does success mean to me?

SET REALISTIC GOALS

"The only limit to the height of your achievements is the reach of your dreams and your willingness to work for them."—**Michelle Obama**

As a Life & Career Coach, I am a fan of setting goals. Setting goals might not work for everyone, but it is always a starting point because to understand how to get somewhere, you need to know where you are going. That is where S.M.A.R.T. goals come in. I am sure you have heard of this principle. According to Wikipedia:

"In their 1981 article "There's a S.M.A.R.T. way to write management goals and objectives," George Doran, Arthur Miller, and James Cunningham used S.M.A.R.T. for management teams and companies. Their method became so popular that it was adapted for personal goals as well."[70]

You might hear of many different interpretations of S.M.A.R.T. goals, but the original method started with: Specific, Measurable, Assignable, Realistic, and Time-related. Then it was changed multiple times to fit personal goal setting, but Realistic seemed to stick. Then I heard of R for Reachable as well.

I don't believe you need to use any of those interpretations because they might actually limit you. Let me explain here a bit more. If you only set realistic or reachable goals, you might never go for something extraordinary, crazy, or impossible. If Elon Musk, Steve Jobs, Henry Ford, Thomas Edison, or Nikola Tesla had ever used this formula, we would lack many great and seemingly impossible inventions nowadays.

What might seem unrealistic today may become realistic and reachable tomorrow.

---

70 "SMART Criteria." In *Wikipedia*, July 19, 2023. https://en.wikipedia.org/w/index.php?title=SMART_criteria&oldid=1166106554.

I like to use this way of setting S.M.A.R.T. goals:

S–Specific

M–Meaningful

A–Action Oriented

R–Rewarding

T–Trackable

Writing and publishing a book was a very unrealistic goal for me just a few years ago—I might have said impossible. But I decided to do it anyway, and I started from what I knew I could do then.

I started by writing two pages daily, then by researching how to edit, publish, and market. Thanks to the internet, we don't need to know everything. We just need to be brave enough to google it and take the time to learn something new. Then, of course, don't forget to use what you learned.

Why It Happens

Many people prefer to stick to realistic and reachable goals. Firstly, they are more achievable, with fewer chances to fail... but fewer chances to learn something new and go beyond your comfort zone. Secondly, achieving a realistic goal brings a sense of satisfaction and accomplishment faster, and we all live in a world where we want everything now and quickly, and if we have to work for it a bit longer, we lose interest.

How To Crack This Wall

How can you make impossible goals possible? You have to convince yourself that you've already reached your goals by thinking, talking, dressing, acting, and feeling like you've "made it." No need to spend a lot of money to match your future self—the best place to start is by fixing your thoughts and feelings, talking, and acting.

You can start by saying something like:

What might seem unrealistic today may become realistic and reachable tomorrow. Just make the first step today.

Ask yourself these questions:

What is my unrealistic goal?

What one step (that I already know how to do) could I take today?

What makes me think this is unrealistic?

How could I make it realistic in six months?

THE EARLY BIRD GETS THE WORM

We all hear this idiom from our parents, especially when they want us to get up early. First of all, studies have shown that kids who sleep a bit longer in the mornings are more productive at school and get better results.[71] Secondly, have you thought of the worm? He apparently woke up even earlier…

We often want our children and ourselves to be first, best, and perfect. I think this is a *perfect* chapter to talk about *perfection*.

Have you ever felt a paradox where the more effort you put into achieving perfection, the less satisfied you feel with the outcome? We often believe that we could have done better, quicker, or with more originality. Despite pouring our heart and soul into a project, we remain dissatisfied. Even minor mistakes that go unnoticed initially seem to fail everything in the end and give us another reason to start over again.

"Perfect is the enemy of good." —**Voltaire**

Honestly, I don't even know what "perfect" means. Is there a guideline or a specific recipe for perfection? And I am not talking about cooking here… a recipe for perfection might work in the kitchen. But when discussing any other project, when do we know it is "perfect"? I think "good" is a sign that you are on the right path.

Why It Happens

Have you ever wondered why you strive for perfection all the time? It's not something that just happens out of the blue. There is probably a reason behind it. Maybe your parents didn't show enough appreciation

---

71 UW News. "Teens Get More Sleep, Show Improved Grades and Attendance with Later School Start Time, Researchers Find." Accessed July 31, 2023. https://www.washington.edu/news/2018/12/12/high-school-start-times-study/.

for your achievements. Maybe other kids seemed to impress your parents more for some reason, or they didn't want to praise you too much for fear of spoiling you?

I have been there. At 15 years old, I came home to tell my father something I was proud of. But he wasn't impressed at all. He said something like, "You could do better," and I blew up... saying that I was never enough for him, no matter what I did and how much I tried to impress him. I think for some time, it had an influence on me, but in the opposite way... I felt like I was never good enough for anything.

Or maybe you used to hear criticism from other people, including teachers, parents, and friends, which made you doubt your abilities? I understand that managing perfectionism can be difficult, but identifying the root cause of the issue can be helpful in achieving a greater sense of inner peace.

How To Crack This Wall

Start by letting go of your projects when you feel they are good enough, not perfect. I love this quote: "Done is better than perfect." I use it often too. Even if I feel I could do better, done is better than not done at all, and I release it into the world. I analyze it later to see if it worked, then maybe I tweak something to improve it.

Remember, the early bird needs sleep, too.

You can start by saying something like:

Done is better than perfect.

Ask yourself these questions:

Where is my perfectionism coming from?

What if I let go of my project not when it is perfect but when it is done?

How do I know when it is perfect?

A FINAL NOTE

Congratulations!

What a journey. First of all, I want to take a moment and recognize you. Yes, you, the person who had the courage to pick up this book, dig deep into your limits, and find those invisible walls to your consciousness. This journey is not easy, and it never will be. With each brick you kick down, the realization crashes over you again and again. After working so hard through one wall, you find it to be connected to another one and another, and the journey might not stop your entire life. But it is worth the effort.

I remember attending the Business Boutique conference and listening to Dr. John Delony's presentation at the end of our three-day event. He said something vital that caught my attention. This was when I realized that we don't come as blank sheets of paper into our adulthood to write anything we want. We come with a paper crunched up into a tiny ball with many scribbles of beliefs and limitations. And before we can write anything personal on it, it needs to be unfolded, straightened, and cleared.

Like many out there, I thought I had a good childhood, nothing to complain about. After listening to his speech, I was crying like a baby from realizing how many bricks I was carrying from generations of my family and how heavy they were. But it was even worse when I understood that if I don't take time to break the walls and unload these bricks, I will pass this heavy burden to my children, and they will build on top of it and put their own bricks there as well.

So I hope you will not be afraid of this journey after reading this book. But proud to be the first possibly in your entire family line to break free of the generational prison of limiting beliefs and trapped emotions.

Remember, the labels we put on ourselves often become true. Keep fighting for your freedom of thinking and feeling, and watch your life improve with every wall you destroy in your mind, heart, and body. And don't forget to love yourself every step of the way.

P.S. I hope you benefit from reading this book as much as I did from writing it. I would be very grateful if you take just a few more minutes of your time and leave me a review on Amazon or Goodreads.

Thank you very much for your support.

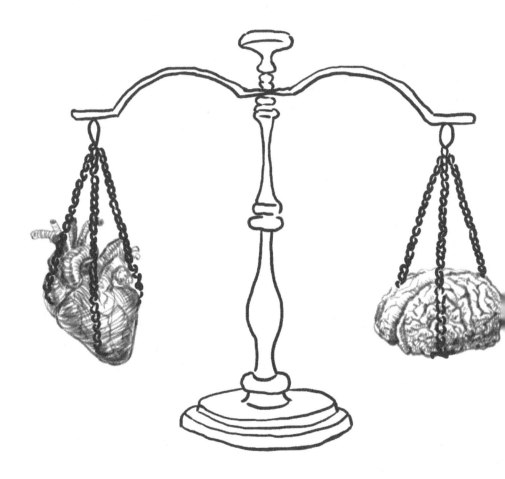

BIBLIOGRAPHY

""7 Famous Entrepreneurs Who Started With No Experience and What Made Them Insanely Wealthy - Finally Family Homes," July 19, 2022. https://finallyfamilyhomes.org/famous-entrepreneurs/.

AARP. "Stories of Famous People Who Turned Their Lives Around." Accessed July 30, 2023. https://www.aarp.org/entertainment/celebrities/info-2017/7-famous-people-who-hit-bottom-and-turned-it-around.html.

American Psychological Association. "The Pain of Social Rejection." Accessed July 31, 2023. https://www.apa.org/monitor/2012/04/rejection.

"Anxiety: What You Need To Know | McLean Hospital." Accessed July 31, 2023. https://www.mcleanhospital.org/essential/anxiety.

Araminta. "Exploring Emotion: Sadness." *Khiron Clinics* (blog), May 22, 2020. https://khironclinics.com/blog/exploring-emotion-sadness/.

Balconi, Michela, Davide Crivelli, and Maria Elide Vanutelli. "Why to Cooperate Is Better than to Compete: Brain and Personality Components." *BMC Neuroscience* 18 (September 20, 2017): 68. https://doi.org/10.1186/s12868-017-0386-8.

"Behavioral Sink." In *Wikipedia*, June 25, 2023. https://en.wikipedia.org/w/index.php?title=Behavioral_sink&oldid=1161835346.

Bourg, Jim. "June Tangney on 'Shame.'" Psychology. Accessed July 30, 2023. https://psychology.gmu.edu/articles/12362.

BusinessDay. "How Painful Emotions Buried Alive Never Die." Businessday NG, January 20, 2023. https://businessday.ng/news/article/how-painful-emotions-buried-alive-never-die/.

Contributors, WebMD Editorial. "All About Anxiety Disorders: From Causes to Treatment and Prevention." WebMD. Accessed July 31, 2023. https://www.webmd.com/anxiety-panic/anxiety-disorders.

"What Is an Entitlement Mentality?" WebMD. Accessed July 30, 2023. https://www.webmd.com/mental-health/what-is-an-entitlement-mentality.

Day, Martin V., and D. Ramona Bobocel. "The Weight of a Guilty Conscience: Subjective Body Weight as an Embodiment of Guilt." *PLOS ONE* 8, no. 7 (July 31, 2013): e69546. https://doi.org/10.1371/journal.pone.0069546.

DeWall, C. Nathan, and Brad J. Bushman. "Social Acceptance and Rejection: The Sweet and the Bitter." *Current Directions in Psychological Science* 20, no. 4 (August 2011): 256–60. https://doi.org/10.1177/0963721411417545.

Dold, Kristen. "What Disappointing News Does to Your Body." *Vice* (blog), December 20, 2016. https://www.vice.com/en/article/bmn3w4/what-disappointing-news-does-to-your-body.

Dukakis, Andrea. "Child Marriage, Common In The Past, Persists Today." Colorado Public Radio. Accessed July 31, 2023. https://www.cpr.org/show-segment/child-marriage-common-in-the-past-persists-today/.

Emotion Typology. "Contempt." Accessed July 31, 2023. https://emotion-typology.com/negative_emotion/contempt/.

Emotion Typology. "Desperation." Accessed July 31, 2023. https://emotiontypology.com/negative_emotion/desperation/.

"Emotional Overwhelm." Accessed July 31, 2023. https://www.goodtherapy.org/learn-about-therapy/issues/emotional-overwhelm.

Everson, S. A., D. E. Goldberg, G. A. Kaplan, R. D. Cohen, E. Pukkala, J. Tuomilehto, and J. T. Salonen. "Hopelessness and Risk of Mortality and Incidence of Myocardial Infarction and Cancer." *Psychosomatic Medicine* 58, no. 2 (1996): 113–21. https://doi.org/10.1097/00006842-199603000-00003.

EverydayHealth.com. "The Destructive Power of Hate," July 26, 2023. https://www.everydayhealth.com/emotional-health/destructive-power-hate/.

EverydayHealth.com. "The Health Risks of Loneliness: What the Science Says," February 25, 2022. https://www.everydayhealth.com/wellness/united-states-of-stress/what-toll-does-loneliness-take-on-our-health/.

"Forgiveness: Your Health Depends on It," November 1, 2021. https://www.hopkinsmedicine.org/health/wellness-and-prevention/forgiveness-your-health-depends-on-it.

Fredrickson, Barbara L., and Christine Branigan. "Positive Emotions Broaden the Scope of Attention and Thought-Action Repertoires." *Cognition & Emotion*, vol. 19, no. 3, May 2005, pp. 313–32. *PubMed Central*, https://doi.org/10.1080/02699930441000238.

"Grief." In *Wikipedia*, July 4, 2023. https://en.wikipedia.org/w/index.php?title=Grief&oldid=1163451399.

"Guilt | Psychology Today." Accessed July 30, 2023. https://www.psychologytoday.com/us/basics/guilt.

"Hardest or Easiest Work First? What the Research Shows - The Productive Engineer," September 18, 2019. https://theproductiveengineer.net/hardest-or-easiest-work-first-what-the-research-shows/.

Hardy, Benjamin. "Why Most People Will Never Be Successful." CNBC, July 14, 2017. https://www.cnbc.com/2017/07/14/why-most-people-will-never-be-successful.html.

Healthline. "Are You Carrying 'Emotional Baggage' Here's How to Break Free," September 16, 2021. https://www.healthline.com/health/mind-body/how-to-release-emotional-baggage-and-the-tension-that-goes-with-it.

Huecker, Martin R., Kevin C. King, Gary A. Jordan, and William Smock. "Domestic Violence." In *StatPearls*. Treasure Island (FL):

StatPearls Publishing, 2023. http://www.ncbi.nlm.nih.gov/books/NBK499891/.

Isaacson, Walter. *Einstein: His Life and Universe.* New York: Simon & Schuster, 2007.

"Jan Koum." In *Wikipedia*, July 23, 2023. https://en.wikipedia.org/w/index.php?title=Jan_Koum&oldid=1166659267.

"Johanna Quaas." In *Wikipedia*, April 20, 2023. https://en.wikipedia.org/w/index.php?title=Johanna_Quaas&oldid=1150882408.

Johansson, Anna. "5 Successful Entrepreneurs Who Started With No Experience But Made Sure They Got It." Entrepreneur, September 13, 2018. https://www.entrepreneur.com/leadership/5-successful-entrepreneurs-who-started-with-no-experience/319971.

Kam, Katherine. "How Anger Can Hurt Your Heart." WebMD. Accessed July 30, 2023. https://www.webmd.com/balance/stress-management/features/how-anger-hurts-your-heart.

Kämmerer, Annette. "The Scientific Underpinnings and Impacts of Shame." Scientific American. Accessed July 30, 2023. https://www.scientificamerican.com/article/the-scientific-underpinnings-and-impacts-of-shame/.

Kellogg Insight. "Why You Should Skip the Easy Wins and Tackle the Hard Task First," November 4, 2019. https://insight.kellogg.northwestern.edu/article/easy-or-hard-tasks-first.

Kuroski, John. "6 World-Changing Inventions You've Been Crediting To The Wrong Person." All That's Interesting, March 7, 2016. https://allthatsinteresting.com/famous-inventors.

"Learned Helplessness | Psychology Today." Accessed July 31, 2023. https://www.psychologytoday.com/us/basics/learned-helplessness.

"Locus of Control Theory In Psychology: Internal vs External," November 3, 2022. https://www.simplypsychology.org/locus-of-control.html.

Maslow's Hierarchy of Needs. 3 Nov. 2022, https://www.simplypsychology. org/maslow.html.

McDowell, Erin. "19 Famous Figures Who Went from Rags to Riches." Business Insider. Accessed July 30, 2023. https://www.businessinsider.com/millionaires-billionaires-who-came-from-nothing-rags-to-riches-stories-2019-7.

Nations, United. "World Population to Reach 8 Billion on 15 November 2022." United Nations. Accessed July 30, 2023. https://www.un.org/en/desa/world-population-reach-8-billion-15-november-2022.

"Neuroscientist Leads Unprecedented Research to Map Billions of Brain Cells." Accessed July 31, 2023. https://www.uchicagomedicine.org/forefront/neurosciences-articles/can-100-billion-neurons-be-mapped.

Pandey, Erica. "Lonely America." Axios Finish Line, n.d. https://www.axios.com/2022/10/26/loneliness-pandemic-america-phone-calls.

"Pareto Principle." In *Wikipedia*, July 31, 2023. https://en.wikipedia.org/w/index.php?title=Pareto_principle&oldid=1168013778.

Penn Today. "Money Matters to Happiness—Perhaps More than Previously Thought," January 18, 2021. https://penntoday.upenn.edu/news/money-matters-to-happiness-perhaps-more-than-previously-thought.

Pert, Candace B. *Molecules of Emotion: Why You Feel the Way You Feel*. New York: Scribner, 2003.

Psych Central. "Effects of Emotional Abuse on Your Brain, Relationships, and Health," March 23, 2022. https://psychcentral.com/health/effects-of-emotional-abuse.

Psyche. "What Makes Hate a Unique Emotion – and Why That Matters | Psyche Ideas." Accessed July 31, 2023. https://psyche.co/ideas/what-makes-hate-a-unique-emotion-and-why-that-matters.

Psychological & Counseling Services. "Resentment and Forgiveness," March 10, 2020. https://www.unh.edu/pacs/resentment-forgiveness.

Psychology Tools. "Resource." Accessed July 30, 2023. https://www.psychologytools.com/resource/.

Ramachandran, Vilayanur S., and Baland Jalal. "The Evolutionary Psychology of Envy and Jealousy." *Frontiers in Psychology* 8 (2017). https://www.frontiersin.org/articles/10.3389/fpsyg.2017.01619.

"Research Statistic on Financial Windfalls and Bankruptcy." Accessed July 31, 2023. https://www.nefe.org/news/2018/01/research-statistic-on-financial-windfalls-and-bankruptcy.aspx.

"Sadhguru." In *Wikipedia*, June 8, 2023. https://en.wikipedia.org/w/index.php?title=Sadhguru&oldid=1159120176.

Silvia, Paul J. "Confusion and Interest: The Role of Knowledge Emotions in Aesthetic Experience." *Psychology of Aesthetics, Creativity, and the Arts* 4, no. 2 (May 2010): 75–80. https://doi.org/10.1037/a0017081.

Singer, Michael A. *The Untethered Soul: The Journey beyond Yourself.* Oakland, CA: New Harbinger Publications, 2007.

"SMART Criteria." In *Wikipedia*, July 19, 2023. https://en.wikipedia.org/w/index.php?title=SMART_criteria&oldid=1166106554.

SocialSelf. "Loneliness Statistics 2022: Demographics, USA & Worldwide." Accessed July 31, 2023. https://socialself.com/loneliness-statistics/.

Team, Changes Psychology. "What Part of the Brain Controls Behavior and Emotions? - Changes Child Psychology Slug." *Changes Child Psychology* (blog), July 13, 2017. https://changespsychology.com.au/brain-emotions-behaviours/.

"Tess Holliday." In *Wikipedia*, July 25, 2023. https://en.wikipedia.org/w/index.php?title=Tess_Holliday&oldid=1167017381.

The Berkeley Well-Being Institute. "Hopelessness: Definition, Examples, & Theory." Accessed July 31, 2023. https://www.berkeleywellbeing.com/hopelessness.html.

The Muse. "9 Famous People Who Will Inspire You to Never Give Up," March 27, 2014. https://www.themuse.com/advice/9-famous-people-who-will-inspire-you-to-never-give-up.

UW News. "Teens Get More Sleep, Show Improved Grades and Attendance with Later School Start Time, Researchers Find." Accessed July 31, 2023. https://www.washington.edu/news/2018/12/12/high-school-start-times-study/.

Verywell Mind. "The Psychology of Fear." Accessed July 31, 2023. https://www.verywellmind.com/the-psychology-of-fear-2671696.

Ward, Tom. "The Amazing Story Of The Making Of 'Rocky.'" Forbes. Accessed July 30, 2023. https://www.forbes.com/sites/tomward/2017/08/29/the-amazing-story-of-the-making-of-rocky/.

Wierzbicka, A. *Cognitive Domains and the Structure of the Lexicon: The Case of Emotions.* Vol. Mapping the mind: Domain specificity in cognition and culture. Cambridge University Press, 1994.

Wierzbicka, Anna. *Emotions across Languages and Cultures: Diversity and Universals.* Studies in Emotion and Social Interaction. Cambridge [England] ; New York : Paris: Cambridge University Press ; Editions de la Maison des sciences de l'homme, 1999.

"'Worry' Is a Useless Emotion! | Psychology Today." Accessed July 31, 2023. https://www.psychologytoday.com/us/blog/the-high-functioning-alcoholic/201906/worry-is-useless-emotion.

ACKNOWLEDGMENTS

Thank you to my friends Irina Lenko, Evgeniya Stetsenko, and Selma Hill. They supported me and helped me to brainstorm the next wall when I felt stuck.

Thanks to my husband, who helped me publish this book and who supports all my crazy projects.

Thanks to my family who always believes in me, no matter what my next impossible mission is.

Thanks to all the great minds who wrote books I learn from daily.

ABOUT THE AUTHOR

Kateryna Armenta was born in Kazakhstan and grew up in Ukraine. Already at 16 years old, she fearlessly stated to everyone that she would be living in the US one day. At the time, no one among her family or friends could believe what this young lady had planned for her life.

She graduated in Ukraine with a financial degree and in Poland with a Quality Control Management degree before traveling the world, working on cruise ships. She traveled to the US for the first time when she was 19 years old and spent a summer in New Jersey working as a lifeguard. When she returned home, the sparkle in her eyes changed forever, and now nothing could stop her.

In 2013 Kateryna decided to move to the United States to settle. She found herself managing condominiums and homeowners associations. After five successful years as Community Association Manager with several certifications and designations, she made a leap of faith to become a life coach and motivational speaker for women to discover their potential and become ambitious boss ladies who take control of their lives.

She got married to her husband, Marco, in 2017 and had her first baby boy in 2020. She continuously learns new things and loves to travel.

She wants to empower women in her community and worldwide to achieve their goals and live the life they deserve.

Now she is the founder of Ambitious WE Life and Career Coaching. She is a certified Life Coach, NLP Practitioner, and HeartMath® Mentor.

Her first book, *I Know What You Need To Succeed*, won the Readers' Favorite Finalist Award in the Non-Fiction - Autobiography category.

She offers one-on-one coaching, online programs, workshops, and public speaking to inspire others.

You can find more information at www.ambitiouswe.com.

ABOUT THE ILLUSTRATOR

Roslaw Rusinov

MEET ROSLAW, a driven artist from Ukraine who always seeks out fresh sources of inspiration. In his teens, he pursued acting and actively participated in organizing and photographing the conceptual photo project UPALA. Roslaw then studied fashion design in Khmelnytskyi and gained extensive experience in the fashion industry. However, his passion for creative expression extended beyond clothing design, and his educational internship in Paris gave him the opportunity to immerse himself in the world of art, which he won through a young clothing designer competition. Over time, Roslaw began exploring new forms of artistic expression beyond fashion design, collaborating with independent writers as an illustrator while also creating his own stunning artwork. He currently resides and works in Kyiv, continuing to create and inspire others with his innovative and dynamic art. You can reach him at roslawr@gmail.com.